ADVANCED PRAISE FOR *SOUNDS OF MOVIES*

Sounds of Movies is a valuable resource for any individual desiring to understand the aesthetic process behind the creation of sound tracks for motion pictures. Many film students discover only belatedly the vital importance of the contribution of audio to the realism and dynamism of a film. By conducting these interviews with the industry's top audio professionals, Mr. Pasquariello has contributed significantly to an understanding of the importance that professional directors, such as Peter Weir, attach to the careful construction of a motion picture's sound tracks. In their own words, these top artists of the field discuss the conceptualization and creation of their work, the process of which will remain similar no matter what the future of technological innovation holds. This book should be read and reread by every serious student of film sound.

Professor J. Duane Meeks
School of Cinema-Television and Theater Arts
Regent University

Nicholas Pasquariello's book *Sounds of Movies* is an invaluable document of pragmatic and aesthetic solutions provided by leading sound mixers and designers of big budget films. It should be of interest both to students who wish to appreciate the creative potential of the sound track and to non-sound film professionals who are less than fully aware of the contributions of their colleagues in post production.

Elizabeth Weis
coeditor *Film Sound: Theory and Practice*
(Columbia University Press, 1985)

To the uninitiated sound mixing is as mysterious an art as film editing. Nick Pasquariello, a contributor to such industry magazines as *Mix, In Motion* and *Studio Sound*, regularly interviews some of the leading mixers in the field. By perusing the dozen conversations featured in *Sounds of Movies*, one can learn much about the complexities involved in various projects: recording *A Chorus Line* in the confines of a Broadway theater; capturing the hard-boiled reality of warfare in *Platoon*; combining the great music and classic acting of *Amadeus*; recreating the sounds of the Twenties and Forties for *The Cotton Club* and *Tucker*; and obtaining theater-quality sound in the sweltering jungles of Central America for *Mosquito Coast*.

Most fascinating are the accounts of recording in China's Forbidden City for *The Last Emperor*; the dangers inherent in capturing the din of the America's Cup race for *Wind*; the weirdness entailed in securing an aura for *Mishima*; and enhancing the period atmosphere of *Tucker*. Discussions examining the ramifications of a global standardization for multimedia production, methods of restoring archival soundtracks, and the preparation of music and effects for foreign release dubs also prove of interest.

George Turner
Book Review Editor
American Cinematographer Magazine

Sounds of Movies: Interviews with the Creators of Feature Sound Tracks is full of valuable insights and information about sound design in film. The way it is structured, concentrating on production sound as well as post production sound mixing, is very effective. Futhermore, interview discussion of specific films make these subjects much more interesting and accessible.

Ece Karayalcin
Assistant Professor
School of Film and Video
Miami-Dade Community College, Florida

The search for knowledge of how film sound works from concept to the finished production is a must for a good filmmaker.

The interviews with the creators of sound for film that you have in your book, *Sounds of Movies*, will go a long way toward inspiring and informing film students how an adequate knowledge of film sound extends well beyond simply the use of a microphone and a recorder. These interviews will help students identify and locate problems with their film sound. It will also greatly assist them in selecting the right location to shoot in and later the best methods to use in mixing their sound tracks.

John L. Butler, Jr., C.A.S.
Manager
Peterson Sound Studio
School of Film
Ohio University

Nicholas Pasquariello's *Sounds of Movies* is a significant addition to a small body of publications related to the art of sound recording. The author has succeeded in bringing together a quantity of high quality information directly from the practitioners of the art of recording. The practical side of audio recording has been a topic of limited discussion in academia. There are few books on the theoretical analysis of the aesthetics of sound. Mr. Pasquariello's book provides a comprehensive, candid and very clear perspective of practitioners' points of view. This book is a timely, down to earth, technical book on sound. What makes this book fascinating is that many recordists have contributed to provide factual and relevant information about the audio medium in a way that both captures and conveys its reality and creativity. This book will be helpful to many media students who deal with audio recording in analysis and production classes.

Vinay Shrivastava
Assistant Professor
Broadcast and Electronic Communication Arts
San Francisco State University

SOUNDS OF MOVIES
Interviews with
the Creators of Feature Sound Tracks

Nicholas Pasquariello

Port Bridge Books
San Francisco, California

This book may be ordered by mail from:

Port Bridge Books
Post Office Box 42791
San Francisco, California 94142
(415) 431-2990

Copyright 1996 Nicholas Pasquariello
 Fourth printing

ISBN 0-9653114-7-3
Library of Congress Catalog Card Number 96-92394

Cataloguing in Publication (CIP) (compiled by publisher)
791.4
sound motion pictures
motion pictures—United States—Interviews

This book is dedicated to my mother and father whose persistence of vision and heart has been a constant inspiration to me.

Contents

INTRODUCTION

In *Sounds Of Movies* eleven of the world's finest sound mixers share their accumulated experiences and techniques which have resulted in the recording and mixing of more than 300 major theatrical features. Their achievements may best be reflected in eight Academy Awards for Best Sound with which these mixers have been honored.

Their *oeuvre* embraces the down-in-the-dirt realism of Oliver Stone's Vietnam-era **Platoon** and the death-defying risks of recording the America's Cup race (**Wind**) to Milos Forman's elegant, period masterpiece, **Amadeus**. From Francis Coppola's idealized portrait of maverick carmaker Preston **Tucker** to Paul Schrader's surreal depiction of writer-terrorist **Mishima**. Two-time Academy Award winner Chris Newman compares **Chorus Line**'s production mixing in the controlled circumstances of a Broadway theater with the challenges of recording theatrical quality pristine sound in the humid, bug infested jungles of Central America (**Mosquito Coast**). Bernardo Bertolucci's production mixer Ivan Sharrock describes the demands of helping create the Academy Award-winning sound track (and first Western theatrical feature) in China's Forbidden City (**The Last Emperor**).

Other issues of continuing interest to film sound professionals and students are the restoration of archival sound tracks and the increasing importance of foreign language dubs, aka foreigns, for the rich American export market.

In many cases the techniques and technologies discussed in this book are appropriate only to the particular film under discussion. Although an attempt was made to list complete credits this was not always possible. The director's name follows date of American release of the picture. Finally, in credit lists a double asterisk (**) indicates the interviewee received an American Academy Award (Oscar) for Best Sound. A triple asterisk (***) indicates a British Academy Award was received. Precis containing major subjects covered precede each interview or chapter. These may be especially useful when this book is used in a classroom setting.

These interviews provide a glimpse into a creative and little understood part of filmmaking, a world the author has been endlessly fascinated with, from a lifelong passion for classical music, the physics and physicality of sound, to a philosophical hunger in finding an Aristotelian unity in the world around us.

Material in this book originally appeared in **Mix, Studio Sound**, the **East Bay Express**, **Lighting Dimensions**, and **Theater Crafts** Magazines.

SECTION ONE

PRODUCTION SOUND

1
A Chorus Line
On location on Broadway

Chris Newman
(part one)

In 1968, an obscure documentary sound recordist by the name of Chris Newman was changing planes at the Los Angeles airport returning from a shoot in India, when he was paged over the PA system. The operator instructed him to call Haskell Wexler. Recalls Newman, "I called Haskell Wexler, expecting this to be some kind of fantasy come true. Wexler said, 'I heard a lot of things about you. I'm doing a movie in Chicago, it's called **Concrete Jungle**. Are you interested?' As he was saying, 'Are you interested?', I was overlapping him and saying, 'Yes, I'm interested.' I would have done it for nothing. It was a feature film. It was Haskell Wexler, who was a hero to me." The picture, later retitled **Medium Cool**, was Newman's first theatrical feature job, and proved to be one of the more successful experiments in the newly invented genre of "docu-dramas." **Medium Cool** indeed marks the point at which Newman made an enormously successful transition from documentary sound recordist to theatrical feature film recordist.

During the past quarter-century he has supervised the location and studio sound recording of 52 feature films under directors the caliber of Coppola, Forman (3 pictures), Friedkin (3 pictures), Ashby, Passer, Pakula (3 pictures), and Attenborough. His peers have publicly acknowledged his achievements as an audio craftsman by awarding him two Academy Awards for Best Sound (for **The Exorcist,** and **Amadeus**).

In the late 1950s, Newman used recording merely as a means to support himself while making short films. (By his own admission, he is largely self-taught in his profession). By the early '60s, he found himself so successful at recording work that he abandoned filmmaking entirely to devote himself to audio work. There followed television and documentary recording jobs such as **Brimstone: the Amish Horse** (for Disney) and an independently produced documentary on Ravi Shankar, filmed in India. When Newman returned from making this film, he met Wexler.

This interview covers the making of the film **A Chorus Line,** directed by Richard Attenborough (perhaps best known for the film **Gandhi**). Largely because of cost (and somewhat unconventionally) **A Chorus Line** was shot in a theater—the Mark Hellinger in midtown Manhattan. As a result of this fact alone, Newman was faced with many interesting (often unique) sound recording situations.

Precis

Recording in a theater, background noise, radio mikes, working with dancers, boom mikes, playback/live recording, music cues, segueing from dialogue to dance recording and back, wireless headphones, dancers doing Foley to their own dancing, recording live dialogue and background playback music simultaneously, use of a digital metronome thumper, compared to click track, earwigs, the efficacy of looping vs. production recording.

Chris Newman's credits

Medium Cool (1969) Haskell Wexler
The Landlord (1970) Hal Ashby
Little Murders (1971) Alan Arkin
The French Connection (1971) William Friedkin
Klute (1971) Alan Pakula
Heartbreak Kid (1971) Elaine May
The Godfather (1972) Francis Coppola
Cops and Robbers (1972) Aram Avakian
Shamus (1973) Buzz Kulik
The Exorcist ** (1973) William Friedkin
The Taking of Pelham 1-2-3 (1974) Joseph Sargent
Law and Disorder (1974) Ivan Passer
Mickey and Nicky (1976) Elaine May
Who'll Stop the Rain (1978) Karel Reisz
Comes a Horseman (1978) Alan Pakula
All that Jazz (1979) Bob Fosse
Hair (1979) Milos Forman
Winter Kills (1979) William Richert
Power (1980) Barry Shear and Virgil Vogel
One Trick Pony (1980) Robert M. Young
Fame (1980) Alan Parker
Ragtime (1981) Milos Forman
Sophie's Choice (1982) Alan Pakula
Soup for One (1982) Jonathan Kaufer
Tender Mercies (1983) Bruce Beresford
Beat Street (1984) Stan Latham
Amadeus ** (1984) Milos Forman
A Chorus Line (1985) Richard Attenborough
Brighton Beach Memoirs (1986) Gene Saks
Dream Lover (1986) Nicholas Kazan
The Mosquito Coast (1986) Peter Weir
Power (1986) Sidney Lumet

Wall Street (1987) Oliver Stone
Married to the Mob (1988) Jonathan Demme
The Unbearable Lightness of Being (1988)
    Phil Kaufman
Second Sight (1989) Joel Zwick
See You in the Morning (1989) Alan J. Pakula
Valmont (1989) Milos Forman
Q & A (1990) Sidney Lumet
At Play in the Fields of the Lord (1991)
    Hector Babenco
The Silence of the Lambs (1991) Jonathan Demme
A Stranger Among Us (1992) Sidney Lumet
Thunderheart (1992) Michael Apted
Mr. Wonderful (1993) Anthony Minghella
Philadelphia (1993) Jonathan Demme
Sommersby (1993) Jon Amiel
Blink (1994) Michael Apted
Nell (1994) Michael Apted
Silent Fall (1994) Bruce Beresford
Copycat (1995) Jon Amiel
Home for the Holidays (1995) Jodi Foster
The English Patient (1996) Anthony Minghella

Would you describe some of the problems you had to solve because you were shooting in a theater instead of on a sound stage?

Mostly problems associated with background noise. The stage was such that there were skylights up above, which were almost impossible to seal up, and noise comes in in any case. There were many shots in the script that call for the street doors on the side of the stage to the street to be open. Fortunately the cameraman only required a light effect out there. And [director, Richard]

Attenborough never really saw people making elaborate entrances from the street. So they built a little house out onto the sidewalk—they got permission from New York City—with double insulated walls, stuff like that. And there were lights inside that house. But the truth of the matter is that no matter how well you construct something like that, there's a point of diminishing returns. And you cannot shut out the noise if there's a lot of noise. It varies from day to day. Wednesdays are the worse days because they're matinee days [the Hellinger Theater is located in the theater district of Manhattan]. And you could tell, if you listen in the background, what day the stuff was shot on.

That didn't go into the picture, though?

Well, mostly we were able to either fit lines in from closer takes, and some stuff was looped. It wasn't perfect and I think we knew going into it that it wasn't going to be like a sound stage. But the tracks that we produced, I thought were pretty good, quite good, as a matter of fact. If we had been on a sound stage it would have been much easier and, probably, other kinds of problems would have arisen. But certainly the one enormous advantage you have working on a sound stage is that you never have any serious background [noise] problems. You might have all kinds of other problems but you don't have background noise.

And that's one of the big problems in mixing a feature film: you try to set up a situation where there aren't jarring changes of background from cut to cut and scene to scene. And the easiest way to do that is not to have any background noise to begin with. We could have elected to wire people with radio mikes to cut down the background substantially. But most of these kids are dancers. Most were wearing very tight outfits, leotards of one kind or another. In many cases they segued from speaking into dancing. And I thought, considering that there were 16 principals plus Michael Douglas, that it was absolutely the wrong way to go in terms of a technique. I thought about it for a long time.

Why was it the wrong way to go?

Because it's too inhibiting. If you're shooting on a set, one of the considerations is money and time. One of the things that I get paid for, in addition to making a good sound track, is to execute my work pretty quickly. And if I'm up there constantly fiddling, adjusting, fixing, specing out faulty noise, moving a transmitter because the camera sees it on somebody twirling around—as the boom man (two boom men, in this case) also is—that's a waste of time.

It unsettles the artist. It makes everybody very nervous and it's a negative way to go. If the people were wearing conventional costumes, then it would have been a very serious consideration. And we did use radios occasionally, when we had to.

So you used boom mikes, then, entirely?

Yes. We used Sennheiser shotguns, for the most part. We used an extra long boom made for television work, which is big and cumbersome, and always in the way, but will permit you to make a big reach, a 16-foot reach. I had two very good boom men: Vito Ilardi and Arthur Bloom, who are both first boom men. I also had a terrific playback operator by the name of Neil Fallon.

When you do a job like this, more so than on a lot of other jobs, you really need to have very skilled people helping you because there are so many elements going on. We did constant playback/live, playback/live;

segueing in and out; music cue after music cue; changing cues, making splices and edits in the tape as we went. And, unless you really have good people, like this fellow, Fallon, or the boom people, you can't do a good job. You look like a total fool.

Would you describe how you did the playback/live?

A song would be sung on stage and then there would be a stop. The actor would speak and it would be recorded live, then the music would continue. In some cases we ducked the playback, meaning we just took it out for those two seconds, and then brought it back in again.

Was there live music on the stage while the singing was going on?

No, unlike other movies that I've done, for example, **Fame** or **Amadeus**, there was no singing recorded live. There were lots of discussions about doing some songs live but ultimately the decision was tempered by the fact that things would only be done live if the respective actors or actresses could not lip synch well.

So, what *was* recorded in the theater?

Only the dialogue.

No dancing either?

Dancing, that's a whole other story. What we did was, while the production was shooting and when some less important things were going on, I went with part of my crew to another theater with John Bloom, the editor, and Jonathan Bates, who's their supervising sound editor, from England. We showed some of the cast people a video copy

25

of various parts of the first and second edited reels of the picture. And they, in fact, did Foleys. We used a wireless headphone system. We played cue tracks for them right from the cut sections. And we recorded their Foleys in stereo at this other theater. And those Foleys will be used in the picture.

What was on the video copy they were looking at?

They could see themselves dancing.

So they did Foley to their own dancing?

Yes, exactly. And even they had trouble remembering their routines! So, if we had brought new people in to do the routines it would have been that much more difficult. And we were lucky enough to find a theater where the acoustics were very similar to the theater we were shooting in.

Have you recorded in theaters before?

Yes, but never an entire picture, I'm happy to say. I hope never to do another picture in a theater because it's very tricky and difficult. The noise problems are such that people look at you and say: "What could you possibly be hearing? We don't hear any noise." They always say that to soundmen, anyway, because everyone knows that soundmen are totally crazed. Well, the truth of the matter is that the noise is there and you don't hear it. It's not like going outside or being in a noisy apartment. What's maddening about the theater is that you could never tell where the noise was coming from! It's a huge space. And, for example, the air-conditioner would go on in an adjacent building to cool off a restaurant and you absolutely go nuts.

How many of these problems did you anticipate?

I predicted the noise. My feeling was that we would get away with it and we did in all but ten percent of the cases. In most situations, in addition to having the directional microphones and people who knew how to handle them, we always had actors who were projecting with a fair amount of voice. They were playing from the stage to Zack, who sits at some distance from the stage. And we could rely on that.

We could also rely on the editorial department to take medium and close-up shot tracks and fit them into extremely wide shots, where people were very, very small in the frame. And since John Bloom, the editor, was cutting as we went, we knew pretty much as we went what we needed, what we didn't need, what was going to be fixed, what wasn't going to be fixed.

When you have that kind of grown-up approach to filmmaking where no one is afraid of what they're doing, then you're in a position to deal very openly and say: "We screwed up on that one but we can use that track in there. And this one we have to loop, and this one will be OK if Rick at the transfer house noise suppresses it." It's only when you have a situation where people are very unsure of themselves or put off things, that it becomes very difficult to figure out what to do.

You say there was no music played in the background while the acting was going on.....

That's not entirely true. What happened was—I don't know if you're familiar with some of the songs in **Chorus Line**—but with some of them there are kind of "vamps" or musical interludes that go on while there are soliloquies. In some cases it's necessary for the actors to hear the tempo

27

to get back into tempo or into key when they begin to sing. But, for the most part, since we want to try to preserve the dialogue of the soliloquies in between, we would either take the playback down to an almost inaudible level and hope that their voices would drown it out, which it did in some cases and it didn't in others, or you'd take it out completely. Mike Tronick, the music editor, would count off stage or wave his hand off stage. Then he would direct the playback operator to bring the playback back in as close to the beginning of the playback cue as possible so we could keep as much dialogue as possible. The way I see it my job is to preserve as much of the live dialogue as I possibly can.

In some cases we would use something called a "thumper," which is basically a digital metronome that, if keyed by a variety of things on the playback track, will keep the tempo of the music and will produce a very, very low-frequency thump on the stage. I went out and I bought some sub-woofers which were mounted on the edge of the stage. It's very upsetting for some people to listen to—it sounds like a heartbeat. What happens is you hear the music, the music goes off, then you hear: "Boomp, boomp." In some cases dialogue was going on and people were dancing to the tempo of the thump. So we had to give the dancers something on the stage [to dance to] because we saw their legs moving and it's very, very hard to fake that kind of dancing unless they have something to motivate them. On the other hand, you don't want to screw up the dialogue totally, by having to loop a three-page scene of dialogue. And if you start to use little earpieces for the dancers, you're talking about 16 earpieces and people running around putting them in, taking them out, putting spirit gum on them so they don't fall out when the dancers turn around.

So the purpose of the thumper is to motivate the dancers?

28

Yes, and to keep them in tempo. Then—and this is all quite hypothetical—in the post production, if you put the music back in on top of the thump, the thump becomes part of the rhythm track of music.

You don't hear it?

You hear it as part of the music so you don't know what it is. Suppose, for example, there was a solitary bassist on the stage and he was playing a very low note in tempo and the dancers were cueing off that low note. Or suppose there was a kick drum and he was just going: "thump, thump, thump," keeping time for them. Suppose, when the thing is in fact mixed, you bring in either a piano or a rhythm section. The minute you bring any kind of music back in, you obliterate the thump. The thump becomes part of the musical elements.

It doesn't interfere?

There are times when it worked and times when it didn't work. Most of the time it worked. We only used it three or four times. From the reports that I get it seemed to work very well. I think it's just another technique for shooting dialogue with music going on.

How would you decide when to use the thumper and when not to?

We made educated guesses. The criteria were could we hear it and how loud was it in comparison to the dialogue? And in a couple of cases, since I was making 2-track recordings because I always work with a stereo Nagra, I was able to take a direct feed from the playback track and feed the playback in on another track and listen to the dialogue rehearsal and listen to the playback to see if I could hear any thump. If I didn't hear any thump or if it was way down under their voices, then we assumed it would work. And it did.

And the other criterion was whether the dancer could keep time to it. See, one of the problems of the thumper is that the attack of the thump on a big stage is not very sharp. It's not like a click track. It doesn't have the bite that the leading edge of the click has. It's very dull. And the only way to make it sharper is to raise the frequency. But the higher the frequency the more audible it is; also you have to make it louder. So somewhere there's a compromise between how high you make it and how loud you make it. Between Jeffrey Hornaday and Mike Tronick and all of us working with the dancers and rehearsing them, we were able get them to be sharp enough in the background, so that they in fact were dancing in tempo and a dialogue was going on in the foreground.

What's the frequency range?

From about 25 Hz to about 400 Hz.

What was the approach to the pre-production planning on *Chorus Line*?

It consisted of discussing with Richard [Attenborough], the music people, and Jeffrey Hornaday things such as: we are going to do this dialogue live; we are going to do this dialogue to playback; we are going to do this line to playback. We are going to try to use the thumper here. We are going to try to use earpieces on "Hello 12," because people have to sing imaginary thoughts when it's not a question of tempo, it's a question of mouthing words while other people are speaking.

30

I must say that in every case Attenborough was very patient and very considerate of our needs when we used the earpieces, the so-called "earwigs," which we used a great deal on **Amadeus** and **Fame**. They are little inductive earpieces; they go in the ear canal and you run a loop of wire around the stage. The wire becomes an analog of a speaker. Anything induced in the loop is picked up in the earwig.

When did you use these earwigs?

It's all right to use the thumper if people are dancing but if people are singing...let's say you have a situation as in the song "Hello 12"; some people are singing while people are speaking. In that case it's not possible to do a playback and a live dialogue recording unless one wants to dub the dialogue. If you use the earpieces, then the people who are singing can hear what they have to mouth the words to to create the impression that they're singing and you can still record the dialogue. And then we decided to use these; I think we put out 12 or 14, that's quite a large number. We only did it once, on that song. We had planned to do it on that song. I had seen rehearsals of it on Saturday and knew pretty much how it was going to be shot, and I knew how many earpieces we'd have to have with us. But the usual happens when you use the pieces: we set up, some of them didn't work, for some of the people it was too loud or too soft. It always takes a few minutes to sort that out. And Attenborough was amazingly patient. Another director would have said: "Forget it, let's move on." He said: "OK. Let's take a few more minutes." I told him what the problems were. And the few more minutes paid off.

Well, the point is it's intended to save you money somewhere else.

31

Yes. And also a certain amount of intangibles because if you cost out what looping costs versus production time, there is no question that looping is cheaper than production time. But there are other elements involved: if you break your neck and have actors break their necks to produce really terrific performances of the moment, why are you bothering if you're going to loop. So, somewhere there is a balance between how much you loop and how much you do live depending on the rigors of the show, the actors and the production requirements.

How much looping did you do?

Less than ten percent. Most of the time we do less than ten percent, you just have to fight. You can't be a soundman and do location work and not be assertive and not fight for good sound tracks.

1
The Mosquito Coast
Location mixing in the jungle

Chris Newman
(part two)

Newman was very desirous of working as location recordist on **The Mosquito Coast** for a number of reasons not the least of which was the team of accomplished filmmakers he would be joining: executive producer Saul Zaentz **(Amadeus, One Flew Over the Cuckoo's Nest)**; line producer Jerome Hellman, **(Midnight Cowboy, Coming Home)**; and perhaps Australia's most distinguished director, Peter Weir **(Picnic at Hanging Rock, The Year of Living Dangerously, Gallipoli, Witness)**.

The Mosquito Coast proved to be arguably the most physically challenging of Newman's career prior to 1986 and perhaps since. The Central American terrain of Belize was always hot, humid, muddy and dusty; there were almost no paved roads. This $17 million film was shot during 19 weeks (17 in Belize, two in Georgia) during the first half of 1986. Newman recorded all the live (synch) sound for **The Mosquito Coast** as well as about six days of effects. In addition, Ken Weston (boom man) and Alan Splet (post production sound designer) recorded location effects at various times during the shoot.

Briefly, the story of **The Mosquito Coast** revolves around the life of an American family who move from Massachusetts to the dense Central American jungle to escape decadent middle-class life in the U.S. and begin life anew in the spirit of early American pioneers.

Newman was the only production department head who was American. The remainder of the crew was predominantly Australian with just a few British and American craftsmen. At Peter Weir's insistence the picture was cut in Australia, but sound editing and looping took place at Zaentz's Fantasy Studios in Northern California.

Precis

Recording in the jungle, exhaustive preparation by scouting location, importance of scouting trip, use of a tripod to mount recording equipment on, recording two-track on location (boom and radio mikes), use of production tracks with dailies, finding correct multitrack mike balance while production mixing for the dailies.

How did you go about planning the location sound recording on *The Mosquito Coast*?

What I thought I would need for that job, which also applies to other jobs, is sophisticated equipment that would be very, very ruggedly packaged and relatively small and portable. I think the first thing I did was to get rid of my older radio microphones—which were a little long in the tooth and not quite up to the most contemporary design ideas—and got a bunch of Micron radio mikes from England. They were in a packaging arrangement with antenna splitters and a little rechargeable battery pack for them, so that I could just plug in a master antenna and hook them up in a fairly straightforward manner. What you want to do to overcome the disadvantages in using radio mikes is to have them available to be working as quickly as possible. I did the same thing with my mixing panels. I got a couple of Sonosax mixers and got rid of the older consoles that I had. Then one of the guys who works with me, Bob Gaulin, modified the Sonosax to make it as sophisticated as the units I was getting rid of, but in a much smaller space and much more state-of-the-art kind of design, and something more suited to a job on the move in the jungle.

I also began to look at packaging of gear in terms of how to carry it: backpacks, bags, waterproofing, all that kind of stuff.

What were your expectations prior to beginning this picture?

I read the script three or four times and I had read the book and I thought the movie would be very difficult, as difficult a movie as I had ever done in my entire life. In the '60s I had worked on documentaries in Southeast Asia and I know what it's like to shoot under hot, jungle-type conditions. No one was going to be shooting at us with bullets but hot is hot and mosquitoes are mosquitoes, mud is mud, dust is dust. It's all the same crap.

What it means is you slog your way through the heat and the dust and stuff and when you get to wherever you're filming, everybody still expects the sound to be perfect. And the problems are exactly the same as if you were walking into a sound studio and making a perfect recording under pristine conditions. The problem is by that time the sweat is running off your forehead down into your eyes, the bugs are banging the shit out of you.

How did the scouting trip to Belize influence your planning of the location recording of *The Mosquito Coast*?

In my chats with Peter and in reading the script I thought that it would be a very good idea to actually go to Central America to see what the locations were like well in advance of the actual shooting. What they normally do is, a week or two before the shooting commences when one is already in place with one's equipment, they take all the heads of departments around and they say, "This is what we're going to shoot here and this is what we're going to shoot here."

On a studio movie or a city-oriented movie in a domestic situation that's time enough. You can say, "We're going to be here in two weeks, have that ice machine shut off and let's control traffic." This is a different situation. I wanted to see the terrain, I wanted to see the boats, I wanted to see as much as they could show me. That scout was as exhausting as the making of the movie and really set the pace for what the movie was like. There was one day when we scouted when we were on foot, we were in vehicles, we were in motor boats—we took a two-hour motor boat ride from the mouth of the river to a small island. We then flew via small plane back to the mainland. All in a ten-hour scouting day.

The point is I got a chance to see every place where they were going to shoot. I was able to see what areas were well organized or when they were still in the process of organizing or when they seemed disorganized. I got to meet the cameraman, John Seale, who is a lovely guy and easy and terrific to work with. And I also got to establish my presence on the movie, which is very important. So already guys in the art department were saying to me, "Well, will that floor be quiet enough or will this be quiet enough?" And in some situations I was able to anticipate, in other situations, even though I saw them,

I was not able to anticipate, because I had no experience in certain kinds of problems.

What kind of microphones did you use?

I used Sennheiser shotguns, the 816s. I used a whole bunch of Schoeps, mostly Colettes and their CK series of hypercardioids. At one point I used the Sennheiser 416 for some pickups that I needed.

Did you work with any new equipment on *The Mosquito Coast*?

We tried a tripod. For years I've been wanting to mount the mixer and the recorder on a tripod 'cause I think it's a great way to work. If you're working on a set in a studio, for example, and you want to be in a corner of the set out of everyone's way, instead of bringing the whole sound cart onto the stage, which sometimes is fine on a ground-level set, they pull a wall out and you're just sitting out there. But suppose the wall or a portion of the wall is in and you want to be able to see to make a fade or to change something— you can't bring your whole sound cart onto the stage, it's absurd. But you could bring a tripod which would be not very much bigger than the profile of the mixer and the recorder. It beats putting it on an apple box and sitting in the corner of the set because you get some elevation and you get a little control over it.

I did a little investigating: I weighed the mixer, I weighed the tape recorder; I added up their weights and added another five or ten pounds for good measure. I went to a professional photographic supply store that sold Gitzo tripods, which is a high quality tripod made in France. I was interested in a low-leg tripod where I wouldn't be expanding the legs to any great degree, that would take 45 pounds of dead weight. I got a set of point legs that would go into the soft earth; and then I had this fellow, Gaulin, who works with me, machine a bottom plate for the mixer that would thread on to the center post of the tripod.

Had you used a tripod before on a studio set?

I never used it anywhere. It works great and I'm going to use it now in other situations where I hadn't anticipated using it. I'm going to use it occasionally on the set.

What effect did the heat and humidity have on the quality of the recordings you made?

It didn't have much of an effect on the equipment. It had a lot of effect on the people. I lost about 15 pounds. I must have made more errors on this movie than on the previous five movies that I worked on put together in terms of throwing the wrong switch or pressing the wrong button and then having to remember that I made a mistake. And I charge a lot of that up to just plain old physical fatigue of schlepping the stuff through the jungle.

Were there advantages to having soundmen on your crew who had also had mixing experience?

Yes. I'll give you an example. We started shooting material that was largely montage, consisting of the building of this town that Allie Fox (the main character) and his family have settled. They build a town from scratch in the middle of the jungle. And there were weeks and weeks of montage filming. There would be isolated little scenes where you would see the family doing specific things: welding, chopping, cutting, finding things to assemble. And some wider shots of all of this activity.

Most of this filming was done with two cameras, which presents a difficult problem for the soundman because you invariably have someone in close-up saying something and you really do want to hear what they're saying. And then you have another camera which is shooting wide. And you don't necessarily hear the same perspective that those people are saying.

Now, if you've got six principals and a dozen supporting players all building this village, it's not possible to wire all of these people. It's a ludicrous idea, especially given the physical conditions. Think of what would have been involved in wiring 18 people, some of whom are not even wearing shirts! And then thinking about, how does one bring a 24-track recorder into the jungle? If one is going to bother to wire there's no point in trying to mix 18 microphones down into two tracks—that's a waste of time given the separation. So what's the next step? Do you go to a 16-track or an 8-track? All of those ideas are out of the question.

So how *do* you do it?

I started out doing it the simplest way possible, where I'm working with the camera guys and Peter Weir and the actors and figuring out who was going to talk, using shotgun microphones and hidden microphones and trying to make it work so that if Allie Harry Fox was walking around speaking very loudly and the microphone was close enough to him that not only would his voice level and quality carry for the wide shot—because the jungle is relatively quiet—that it would also carry for the closer shot.

After some of that filming the results that we were getting using open microphones were not entirely satisfactory because we were not getting enough detail on Harrison Ford. And Kenny [Weston, boom operator],

39

whom I had talked to about this before we started shooting, came to me and said: "Listen, I know you want to do it the simplest way possible, but there are times that we're losing stuff that we don't have to lose. So why don't you think about using two tracks and putting a radio mike, for example, on Harrison and if we get stuff that's garbage we'll throw it away, we won't use it. And we'll still preserve the simpler technique at the same time." Because it turned out in practice as the filming developed, as the acting developed, as Peter's concepts developed, that Harrison Ford was doing most of the talking during the construction scenes.

So that's an example of someone who has a lot of mixing experience in addition to booming experience making a suggestion that was terrific. A lot of people in that situation would have said: "Well, I know the right way to do this, but I'm not going to tell him because I'm just the boom man, I'm not the mixer." But that was not the case. The guy transcended any of those feelings. And he **is** a mixer now.

And what would happen to the mixed tracks? Would they be used for dailies?

Yes, we would transfer to full coat and we would have three different tracks on it: an A, B, and A plus B. And they would cut with the A plus B.

Was Peter hearing these for the dailies?

For the dailies they would hear a mixed track if it was necessary. We would decide at the time of transfer what we would give them for dailies: A only or B only or A plus B; and in what proportions, as well.

Is this common practice in your experience?

It is common practice when making multitrack recordings; it's not common practice when one is not making a
multi-channel recording.

How long have you been working this way?

This is the first time I did the dailies on location but
it's not the first time I did 2-track stuff. I've been doing 2-
track stuff for almost 13 years now.

**Is it unusual for the director to be hearing a pre-mix
with the dailies?**

No, it's not so unusual, in fact ever since we started
doing multitrack work, every other day the director is
hearing one kind of mix or another. I've been doing it in
different amounts. It depends on the needs of the picture. It depends on how willing people are to accept that
technique. There was a time when the editors were very
loath to deal with multitrack techniques. They found it
very confusing and it took a long time for them to break
down their natural resistance to those kinds of things.

**Would you give me some examples of when you
would do a pre-mix for the dailies compared to scenes
for which you would not do a pre-mix?**

It depends on how the results went. For example, if
you're running a lavalier radio mike on Harrison and an
open mike for the rest, and you discover when playing
the material back that having a small amount of Harrison's
voice in the very wide shot to emphasize his character
seemed appropriate, we would make a mix. A couple of
times we made mistakes. There was one situation which

41

was hilarious, where we made Harrison predominate in a scene where he shouldn't have predominated because we were too far away from him, and I thought it was the right balance. And in fact, technically it was the right balance for the size of the shot. But in the rushes Peter came to me and he got very upset and he said, "It's too loud! It's too loud!" I said, "We'll do it again and we'll remix it." He just didn't want to hear Harrison that loud. But the beauty of that system is you go back in and rebalance and you can make it as loud or as soft as you want to make them.

How do you know what the director intends the audio emphasis of the scene will be?

You don't. If you're talking about making a mix that's exactly appropriate to the picture, you cannot do that. So you do guesswork. You're only doing something for the cutting copy. You're not doing it as a final mix. Obviously it's going to be remixed during the rerecording and if those tracks remain in the picture—in this case there are a dozen of those tracks that are still in the picture—they will go to the mix with the full coat and they'll have three strands laid out: A, B, and A plus B. And Mark Berger will remake that balance according to whatever Weir wants in terms of the picture.

If we could go back to your example with the tight shot on Harrison and the wide shot on 17 people—if you've got two cameras running simultaneously you don't know at any given point whether they're in for a close-up or they're out for a wide shot, and you also don't know whether Harrison is going to be loud or soft.

No, we don't, but we would ask the second camera guy—the tighter camera—"What size were you?" And he might say, "I was a bunch of sizes but mostly I was this size; I was medium shot size." Or "I was a big head close-up." Let's say on take one the guy says "Well, he was full figure." So I might say, "OK, Richard for take one just combine both tracks full level so he sounds like he's close but not too close. But on take two or the next number of the setup when they go to a big head close-up of him for the 'B' camera just take the radio mike track only, and for the 'A' camera, which might be wide, take a combine that was similar to take one with both tracks at 100 percent." It's all guesswork. The point is that it doesn't really matter if you guess wrong. What matters is that you have the flexibility to change it.

2
Wind
Location sound at sea

Drew Kunin

Precis

Recording high speed America's Cup theatrical feature at sea under grueling water drenching conditions, methods for keeping equipment dry and functioning.

By far the most adventurous scenes in Carroll Ballard's $30-million America's Cup theatrical feature **Wind** are the racing sequences: about one-third of the picture. Like all good things in life they came at a price, which included the accidental loss of a leg of one of the stuntmen. [Ballard is best known for two ground/back-breaking location pictures, **Never Cry Wolf** (1983) and **The Black Stallion** (1979)].

The racing boats used for location shooting off the coast of Fremantle, Australia, and later Hawaii and Newport, Rhode Island, were eminently well suited for sailing and almost completely inappropriate for filming purposes. "With no hand holds or lifelines [the boats] were not designed for any kind of comfort at all," remarks a member of the crew. The most difficult part of filming was staying on board the 13 X 60-foot racers in 25-knot winds. As Ballard so succinctly put it, "These are danger-ous, mean boats, where the crew has to be filming with-out being killed or decapitated. They can't move around freely because there's half-inch steel cable whipping across decks with 50,000 pounds of pressure on it. It's murder."

Production recordist Drew Kunin spent nearly all of his three months on deck...underwater. "I expected that we would shoot more [theatrical type] setups than we ended up shooting," he says. "We did a lot of stuff from the hip. It was just the sailors and the four of us on the boat. We went through endless maneuvers. Largely in an improvisational fashion, Ballard would set up a task such as a spinnaker set or a tacking operation.

"And then Carroll and John [Toll, the director of pho-tography] would find new camera positions," Kunin con-tinues. "Carroll would be shooting close-ups on Matthew [Modine] at the wheel, while John was shooting the grind-ers. So I was all over the place. In the end I simplified everything and the challenges were less technical than they were physical.

"I wired the boat much the same way one would wire a studio," he adds. "Since most cable is waterproof, the problem comes with the connectors. I ended up using condoms to seal them. [Non-lubricated ones were very difficult to find in Fremantle]. By the time the shoot was over, I changed the connectors several times because of corrosion and rust; I had to keep cutting them and sol-dering new ones on."

As would be expected at sea, miking was at best diffi-cult. What worked the best? "Schoeps CMC4U [preamp] in a Rycote Zepplin with the foam baseball windscreen inside the Zepplin, which is not normally done," Kunin says. "And then I had the Windjammer outside the Zepplin. Then I had a waterproof cover over them, which I would remove before the takes. I had about four

Windjammers with me, which I would constantly change to shake the water out of them.

"I had waterproof pouches made for the radio mikes and waterproof covers made for the Nagras," he continues. "Everyone who's seen the waterproof Nagra and DAT covers has coveted them desperately. You can't get one because no commercial manufacturer makes them. The cover I made looks like a waterproof Nylon shirt with no neck hole. And where the neck hole would be there's a flexible plastic window. On the ends of the arms there are neoprene cuffs so you can stick your hands through the arms and they seal, like the way a dark room changing bag works. At the bottom where the arms go, there's Velcro where you rolled it up three times, flipped it back over and clipped it, like what you do in a dry sack that goes in a kayak, which is where I stole the closure idea from.

"Then I had two clips. One on the inside that I hung the Nagra from, then a clip on the outside that I attached to, so there was no actual sewn through place. That way I could record standing in the rain," he explains. "You just can't do that with any commercially available Nagra cover. I got hundreds and hundreds of gallons of saltwater poured all over me. The Nagra never went down, though I lost a couple of Schoeps when Matthew went overboard a couple of times.

"I strapped myself to my equipment by way of a quickrelease, because if I went overboard attached to this anchor [his sound gear], there would have been no way to stay afloat, even with my life preserver," Kunin notes. "I wired all three boats so I could put two time code Nagras in a box down below [deck] to remote roll them. It involved an immense amount of wires all over the boats. It was very difficult to remote roll the Nagras properly because they needed this big 10-second run-in [The timecode that the EditDroid required in post-production, which

Kunin finally got reduced to five seconds], which was the longest time on Earth."

As one of the assistant directors pointed out there was no way any conventional Hollywood production record-ist—with his chest high metal-cart-on-wheels—could have handled this assignment.

"The funny thing was that I thought I would end up with a much slicker, hi-tech setup, and I ended up revert-ing to documentary style," Kunin laughs. "Carrying ev-erything on me gave me more flexibility. Since the guys tended to project their voices well, I discovered that my best bet was with the boom. I originally had this idea of planting microphones—Carroll really wanted micro-phones planted all over the boat—so that I would not be intrusive and he could run around shooting anything. I tried to comply with this but it didn't work.

"I could get good camera perspective by booming from underneath," he continues. "And an open mike sounded much better on the boats than radio mikes or plant mikes. This was because the boat was a rather quiet sound space; you don't hear the wind so much [using a windscreen], although there is a great wind. When you get anyone speaking loudly—really projecting or yelling—a radio mike (lavalier) tends to overmodulate, and the compres-sor clamps it down and it sounds very flat.

"You don't get any perspective," Kunin concludes. "I would end up lying on the deck underneath the actors, lying in water over my head because the cockpit would fill up with huge waves."

Drew Kunin's credits

That Was Then, This is Now (1985)
Christopher Cain
Down by Law (1986) Jim Jarmusch

Hard Choices (1986) Rick King
Down Twisted (1987) Albert Pyun
Slamdance (1987) Wayne Wang
Tough Guys Don't Dance (1987) Norman Mailer
Haunted Summer (1988) Ivan Passer
Eat a Bowl of Tea (1989) Wayne Wang
Manifesto (1989) Dusan Makavejev
Mystery Train (1989) Jim Jarmusch
The Ballad of the Sad Cafe (1991) Simon Callow
The Comfort of Strangers (1991) Paul Schrader
Night on Earth (1992) Jim Jarmusch
Wind (1992) Carroll Ballard
The Secret Garden (1993) Agnieszka Holland

3
The Last Emperor
Location recording the first major Western feature shot in China

Ivan Sharrock

On the day before he won the Academy Award for Best Sound, location mixer Ivan Sharrock felt his chances for winning the top sound film award to be "very mixed." **The Last Emperor** capped a nearly 30-year career that began at a British Broadcasting Corporation documentary unit—where, as he puts, it if you didn't get the sound you didn't get the picture—and included early training as an electronic engineer.

During the mid-'60s he travelled the world recording sports remotes—in Britain they're called "outside broadcast"—and foreign affairs sound tracks for Alan King Associates, the National Broadcasting Corporation (USA), National Educational Television (USA), and the Canadian Broadcasting Corporation.

When he and his crew arrived in China to work on **The Last Emperor** they initially found accommodations difficult. After being put into a depressing late-'50s, Russian-built monolithic hotel in downtown Beijing, Sharrock's wife discovered an I. M. Pei-designed hotel 45 minutes from the Forbidden City in an idyllic place called "the Fragrant Hills." The daily commute was a long one, but well worth the rural change of pace it provided.

For four months of location recording Ivan Sharrock's crew consisted of himself and two sound assistants, who were alternately British or Chinese. To be sure of having

51

everything with him halfway around the globe from his London home base, Sharrock brought 79 cases of hardware valued at about $160,000 and weighing over 2,000 pounds. For maximum flexibility, especially in situations where no setup was possible, Sharrock used Schoeps stereo microphones with windscreens. On his stereo Nagra he customarily uses 7-inch reels, assuring that he will virtually never leave the camera crew waiting for him to change reels. His tape stock of choice is Agfa-Gevaert PEM 468, which he finds has excellent non-print-through capabilities.

Precis

Preparation and special requirements for shooting in remote China location, director Bernardo Bertolucci's production methods.

Ivan Sharrock's credits

The Dogs of War (1980) John Irvin
The Shining (1980) Stanley Kubrick
American Werewolf in London (1981) John Landis
The French Lieutenant's Woman *** (1981)
        Karel Reisz
Krull (1983) Peter Yates
Greystoke: the Legend of Tarzan, Lord of the Apes
        *** (1984) Hugh Hudson
Spies Like Us (1985) John Landis
The Last Emperor (1987) Bernardo Bertolucci
Ishtar (1987) Elaine May
Willow (1988) Ron Howard

The Sheltering Sky (1990) Bernardo Bertolucci
King Ralph (1991) David S. Ward
Far and Away (1992) Ron Howard
Once Upon a Crime (1992) Eugene Levy
Patriot Games (1992) Philip Noyce
Swing Kids (1993) Thomas Carter
The Little Buddha (1994) Bernardo Bertolucci
Mary Shelly's Frankenstein (1994) Kenneth Branagh
The River Wild (1994) Curtis Hanson

What did you do to prepare for this shoot?

I knew we were going to be in China from late July
(1986) until the middle of November, and then coming
back to Cinecittà studios in Rome, shooting there and on
location in Italy possibly for another two months.

So I went to Rome to sort out what transfer and sound
facilities existed there, and was extremely disappointed
in what I came across, I think basically because I am used
to having access to really good equipment and people who
understand what's going on. It wasn't just the language
problem, it was the way things were done. I happen to
record twin-track and transfer it to triple-track [35 mm.]
on most of the movies that I do. I use a stereo Nagra and
transfer the left track to track two on a triple-track, the
right track to track three, and a combined track for rushes
and editing to track one.

At Cinecittà I discovered, yes, they could triple-track.
I said: "All right, where is the machine you would be doing it on?" They said: "We'll put a chair in here and the
stereo Nagra is set up on the chair." This was in the sound
projection area of one of the dubbing theaters with the
noise of projectors and everything else going on around!
It wasn't the sort of little transfer suite that I am normally
used to.

53

Well, I went back to the producer of **The Last Emperor** in London and said: "I would suggest that we take our own transfer machine to China and that one of my crew do the transfer on location; it will save you the transportation costs of sending the sound back. If there is a problem, we will know what it is immediately; we are here—there's not going to be a communications or customs problem. And we'll take all the 35 mm. stock with us." Which indeed is what we did.

I took a transportable Magnatech 35 mm. triple-track deck to China. It's a machine that uses 35 mm. full coat "between the perf" or clear edge stock. I've taken these all around the world and used them, for example, on **Ishtar** in Morocco and on **The Dogs of War** in Belize.

The editors had their complete sound track on track one anyway, so it would play on any normal "set mag" projectors. You didn't have to have a triple-track projector, when they were showing rushes.

We had portable projectors with us but at the Beijing studios we were using some very good Chinese projectors called Pearl River projectors. I was very impressed with the quality of the picture and sound.

Now I had to work out what we would be needing in China, because we would be going there for so long, and obviously once one is there, there is no way you're going to get any other equipment there in a hurry. We had to prepare and get everything there in one go.

What else was involved in the pre-production planning?

I got a very experienced crew, who have been with me a long time. I had a lot of difficulty in persuading the producers to budget two assistants for me. They were quite sure—again I think because of the Italian connection—that one could do a picture like this with just one assistant. [Because of the common Italian practice of shooting picture without live synch recording, Sharrock had some difficulty convincing the producer to allow for a second sound assistant]. I was adamant in pointing out that [director] Bernardo [Bertolucci] was going to shoot with two cameras a lot of the time, which can make it extremely difficult in booming. I was obviously going to need a multi-mike technique simply to cope with two cameras. Under their initial budget there would have been only two of us.

I did persuade them but not until I got to China. It was a very tricky thing with the producer and the Italian production, who were handling the money. It was quite hard to persuade them that this was necessary, which I found quite frustrating. I've not had this situation before.

How did you work with Bertolucci?

Bertolucci is extremely sound-conscious. He takes his inspiration from the day. He moves the camera a lot. He designs the first shot and from there he will then design the second shot. It's not as if he comes in and says: "Right, there's a wide shot here, we'll then go into a couple of close-ups on that line, back to a two-shot and out." He doesn't work that way.

So it was very difficult to know what his next shot was going to be. You might be on an extremely tight close-up at the end of a long track, having started on a 20 mm. or 18 mm. wide angle encompassing a complete ballroom and ending up on somebody's tight head, and the next shot would be back on 18 mm. again.

We never knew where we were going, so what we tried to do was keep the sound very fluid so you didn't end up with horrendous cuts. What it did necessitate a lot of the time were hidden microphones, some radio mikes. We

55

usually got away with fixed open mikes or boomed mikes—either under or over.

Vittorio's [Storaro, cinematographer] lighting was very easy to deal with: it's a very soft lighting. If one was doing an interior, there were very few lights in a room; everything was outside, as if the light was the natural light of that room, maybe with the odd lamp bounced on a little poly to get a little fill. One of the advantages of this lighting technique is that there were no shadow problems.

The biggest problem that we had all the time was the way that Bernardo would design a shot: there would be no cut-ins on a lot of his shots. You might be on an 18 mm. with somebody right down to the far end of the room. Often I found myself mixing as that person approached, [somebody might be talking from the other end of the room] you'd come across from the radio mike across to the open mike as they got into a tight two-shot.

How would you sum up your working relationship with Bertolucci?

We got on extremely well; we were very sympathetic. He is a man who first and foremost is a poet and a film-maker, as opposed to a director. He has extraordinary facets to his directorial abilities inasmuch as he creates the whole idea of the image from every aspect, including—very much—sound. He's an incredibly sound-conscious director. He is possibly the only Italian director who insists that everything be as it should be on the day [of shooting]; he will not turn over [roll film] unless the sound is right.

4
Platoon
Bringing the battle home from location

Simon Kaye

More than a year before shooting started, the British production recordist, Simon Kaye, got a call in London from an American production company he had never worked for before, Hemdale Productions, inquiring if he would be interested in working on a Vietnam war film entitled **Platoon**. "I was excited and thrilled by the call and asked 'Why me?'" says Kaye.

The call had come just a few weeks before production was to start. "I didn't get out to the Philippines until about four days before we were about to start shooting," Kaye says. "It was tighter than I would have liked." Perhaps the considerable challenge of the shoot was evident from the start. "One of the biggest problems when I got there was that my equipment that came from England was held in bond in customs for rather a long time." So long that Kaye missed the first shot on **Platoon**.

Kaye was the only Englishman who headed a production department on the crew of **Platoon**, which may be part of the reason, perhaps, he was surprised to get the unsolicited call to work from the States. The assignment, though, had a major hitch: he was not allowed to bring his own boom man—a regular part of any location recordist's team—probably because of the film's relatively modest budget (about $10 million).

In 1962, Simon Kaye was doing film sound work for

the Rank Organization at the Pinewood Studios outside of London. There followed assignments on two of the better-produced British TV series, **The Avengers** (40 episodes) and **Human Jungle**. Since then he has been location recordist for a good many of the major European and American directors currently producing theatrical features. His credits number no fewer than 36 theatrical films since 1967, four British Academy Award nominations, two American Academy Award nominations, two British Academy Awards and one American Academy Award.

This interview was conducted the day before Simon Kaye received his American Academy Award for Best Sound on **Platoon**. Asked what he thought his chances of winning were, he responded, "I'm always pessimistic about these things. It's my third attempt [at the American Academy Award]. People say things go in threes."

Precis

Recording a realistic war picture (dialogue and gunfire) under live battlefield-like conditions, innovative use of helmet mikes to obtain 100% pickup area, competing with heavy background noise; inappropriateness of boom mikes, recording rain generated by nearby heavy-duty pumps, live audience tracks.

Simon Kaye's credits

Accident (1967) Joseph Losey

Charge of the Light Brigade (1968)
  Tony Richardson
A Lion in Winter (1968) Anthony Harvey
Brotherly Love (aka **Country Dance**) 1969
  J. Lee Thompson
Oh! What a Lovely War (1969) Richard Attenborough
Macbeth (1971) Roman Polanski
Sunday Bloody Sunday (1971) John Schlesinger
Young Winston (1972) Richard Attenborough
Delicate Balance (1973) Tony Richardson
The Offense (1973) Sidney Lumet
Theater of Blood (1973) Douglas Hickox
Three Musketeers (1974) Richard Lester
Abdication (1974) Anthony Harvey
Juggernaut (1974) Richard Lester
Brannigan (1975) Douglas Hickox
Four Musketeers (1975) Richard Lester
Royal Flash (1975) Richard Lester
The Adventures of Sherlock Holmes' Smarter Brother
  (1975) Gene Wilder
A Bridge Too Far (1977) Richard Attenborough
Jesus of Nazareth (1978) Franco Zeffirelli
  (TV feature)
Eagle's Wing (1979) Anthony Harvey
Yanks (1979) John Schlesinger
Raiders of the Lost Ark (1981) Steven Spielberg
Reds (1981) Warren Beatty
Gandhi (1982) Richard Attenborough
Never Say Never Again (1983) Irvin Kershner
Gorky Park (1983) Michael Apted
Indiana Jones and the Temple of Doom (1984)
  Steven Spielberg
D.A.R.Y.L. (1985) Simon Wincer
Haunted Honeymoon (1986) Gene Wilder
**Platoon ** (1986) Oliver Stone
Cry Freedom (1987) Richard Attenborough

Mountains of the Moon (1990) Bob Rafelson
Meeting Venus (1991) Istvan Svabo
The Last of the Mohicans ** (1992) Michael Mann
Shadowlands (1993) Richard Attenborough

What were the special requirements of recording location sounds for the movie *Platoon*?

Because Oliver [Stone, director of **Platoon**] was so desperate to have this film as natural as possible, he was insistent that explosions and gunfire and anything that was part of the scene, wherever possible, would actually be going on whilst we were shooting the dialogue. From the point of view of performance, he felt it was necessary to the other actors that they knew what was going on off stage. I had to battle in those occasions, because if the actors were not in vision of the camera, I had to try to convince him that they should not be on the sound track. Of course those occasions become slightly heated at times because there are two conflicting views there: you have the director's view and then you have the soundman's view. We managed to make it work because we had an arrangement: he trusted me, I trusted his requirements. And we then attempted to get the best of both worlds.

The film was quite difficult from the point of view of having to shoot live dialogue and also have guns and explosions going on at the same time. And on those occasions I sometimes had to mix the mikes that I was using because if I was able to pot down the condenser mike that I usually use for the dialogue, I would then bring up a dynamic mike for the explosion. And then I was able to hold them. Otherwise, to try to record an explosion or gunfire—depending on its velocity—you may have a lot of problems with a condenser microphone.

Were you switching off from one mike to the other?

Well, I was mixing, yes. All of our actual effects were recorded on a stereo Nagra. My original dialogue recording was all done on a monaural Nagra.

What mikes were you using?

AKG condenser mikes for the dialogue and AKG dynamics for the explosions.

What sounds did you record on location in the Philippines?

Needless to say, the jungle sounds were readily available. But there were also village sounds, of children and general atmosphere for that sort of terrain. Those sorts of things are all needed ultimately. And then, of course, the major parts of the film, since it's a war picture: the movements through the jungle and whatever vehicles are available. I recorded as many sound tracks of those as I possibly could. I always shoot direct [synch] sound on everything, even if the sound track is going to be remade later. Purely from an editing point of view it's very boring not to have any sort of sound track to edit with.

And then as far as gunshots and the AK-47s and all the various armaments for the film, of course we were shooting with blanks when we were actually filming, but then I had someone brought over from England to go off for two weeks to record quite a lot of available live ammunition. Unfortunately, even that didn't work out in its entirety. They only gave us permission to shoot on firing ranges and inevitably while we were on the firing range, the local army was also there so we had a certain amount of interference from extraneous noise that we didn't particularly want.

A war picture is not an easy picture to handle. Also don't forget we had a lot of Filipinos on the crew, who were all marvelous, but there were certain language barriers. They don't have the Western energy, if you like, of American and British technicians. We work very long hours at a pretty high pace. The Eastern countries, I find, probably because of the heat, probably because there's "always **mañana**," don't have the same sort of attitude of being able to rush around in that sort of climate. The temperature was about 100 degrees plus about 90% humidity.

Did you communicate with the post production crew before you began shooting?

No, because those sort of people are not even on the payroll, they've not even been chosen at that point. Sometimes they are. Although in this case we knew who the [supervising] sound editor was going to be—Gordon Daniel. He was not available and he was not engaged on the film until after we'd finished shooting. So he just had to deal with the material that I presented him with. I did have a conversation with him before we finished shooting because I decided that there was no way that I wanted to leave the Philippines with big gaps in the sound track, namely, explosives and gunfire. I also had numerous discussions with the picture editor, Claire Simpson, who was on location with us.

Strangely enough I think what tends to happen with some of us soundmen is that we take on whatever sort of role we decide we want to take on. My interest is the final sound track. And in some cases I know that some people are mainly conscious of what they have to do on each particular day and just fulfill that function.

But you tend to think of your role as wider than that?

I tend to take full responsibility or like to take full responsibility.

Have you a sense of how much of the final sound track was originally recorded on location versus added later in post production?

The editors told me that there was absolutely no looping on the film. All my dialogue production sound was used. All of the dialogue tracks used in the final track were recorded live in synch on location.

Some production recordists participate in various stages of the post-production process such as ADR. Did you?

No, because in this particular instance we left the film in the Philippines, I went to London and they brought the film to L.A. And there was no way that I was available—other than by telephone—to be of assistance because I then immediately went on to the [Richard] Attenborough film [**Cry Freedom**] and we then went on to Africa.

What was the most challenging aspect of doing location recording on *Platoon*?

I suppose not having one's own crew initially is slightly more demanding because however good they are, you always feel that perhaps you ought to be looking over their shoulder to make sure they are going about it in the right way. I feel when I have my own crew with me I'm able to relax so I can perhaps stroll away from the set and have a cup of coffee without being concerned about what's going on back on the set. In this case, once I'd realized that my boom man was absolutely marvelous, I didn't have those sorts of worries.

In addition, there is a lot of dialogue which is of paramount importance to get over as cleanly as possible. Trying on occasion to work when you sometimes have widish angle lenses obviously is a problem as far as getting the boom in the right position. I devised a system in 1976 when I was doing **A Bridge Too Far**, which was also a war film, to use radio mikes I taped into the helmets wired to a transmitter. And that way you don't have body rustle or movement. And of course on a war film, when you have people with webbing and packs that are all rubbing together, I find it's pretty impossible to put a mike on the body.

What kind of microphones were those?

They are the small electrets that we call "Trams."

Did you have any problems with them?

The only problem occurs when the actor wants to take his helmet off. If you have someone in the middle of a scene who wants to take his helmet off and you can't wire him up then you have to think of an alternative. I must say Tom Berringer [one of the film's stars] was absolutely marvelous. He loved the idea. All he did was hand us his helmet, we put his mike and cable into it, we put his transmitter into one of his backpacks and we never had to fiddle with him. I think one of the problems with radio mikes is that you have to fiddle with the actors and it can become very distracting for them.

The beauty of putting the radio mike into a helmet is that when you swing your head from side to side you're actually taking the mike with you so you don't have any loss. What happens if you've got a microphone in a fixed position on the body and you swing your head from left to right, you go through the good pickup area and go out of it. So from that point of view you're able to keep a much more continuously acceptable sound track.

Did you have helmet mikes on all of the main actors?

Only as and when required. I evaluate scene by scene, I don't say, "Well, this is how we're going to shoot the film from the word go." I watch a rehearsal and decide how we can get the best possible sound track. The main reason for going into helmet mike mode in the first place is either because of heavy background noise or because the width of the camera lens won't enable the boom to be where you want it. In many cases we were able to get into a reasonably good mike position and consequently avoided the necessity for the radio mikes.

How much of the dialogue was recorded using radio mikes compared to a boom mike?

Minimal. I tried desperately not to use radio mikes. If I had to put a percentage on it I would say five percent They will not help you a great deal if you've got someone firing guns and playing dialogue at the same time. The mike is going to be on top of the gunfire as is an open mike. So the only thing you can do is to evaluate which mike is going to get you the best possible dialogue pickup and go for it.

Were there instances when Stone was willing to sacrifice the background sounds for the dialogue during synch recording?

We were never so bold as to say we were going to sacrifice. Even in recording the heavy rain sequences—which were extremely difficult to cope with in themselves—the major problems did not arise from recording the rain sounds themselves, but from the fact that the rain had to be pumped by fire engine, and for that you have to use heavy pumps, so you have mechanical noise to try to hide. What we tried to do in those instances was to get those pumps as far away from the set as possible, baffle them as much as possible and get your mike pickup as close to the dialogue as we possibly could.

Although before we started shooting I was very concerned about the rain sequences a lot of them were finally done synch sound. Oliver never really said, "Let's sacrifice." On one or two occasions he said to me, "Look, I'd really like to bring a helicopter in the back of this shot, is it going to murder you?" And I said, "I don't think you should suffer. I think we should go for that because it's visually a very good effect. Let's go for it and we'll re-record the dialogue." He gave me the option. I could have said, "No, let's go for this dialogue and I'll put a sound track of a helicopter on stage." But it was much more agreeable pictorially to see the helicopter.

Is it fair to assume that there were occasions when you were not given an option?

There were occasions when there was gunfire and explosions, some of which were in picture and some of which by necessity had to be off stage for effect. Some of those explosions gave us a visual effect as well: they either lighted up the sky or they lighted up the faces of the actors. And on those occasions we had to accept that they were going to interfere with the sound track.

What film has been your most challenging picture?

Probably **Gandhi**, which is also one of my proudest

sound tracks. The demands were enormous, mostly because of the extraneous noise, most of which we didn't want on the original sound track. It's very difficult when you're confronted with a question like that. I can go way back to **A Lion in Winter**, which we shot in 1968. We did not loop one word of dialogue. I've done that a couple of times. We worked very, very hard. It was a period film: 11th or 12th Century.

Where was it shot?

We shot a lot of it in Ireland on a stage and on location and about 40% in monasteries in the south of France.

To what would you attribute such successful synch location recording?

I think the actors to a great degree. They were so orchestrated in their dialogue that even if we had to replace their sound track—and we did it immediately afterward—they were able to replay their scenes without any problems. The director [Anthony Harvey] also was adamant that we didn't loop.

I wonder if some of the credit might be attributed to the fact that you were often shooting in quiet monasteries?

Well, no, because in those situations the echo was quite great. I did another film [**Abdication**] with the same director, again in those sorts of conditions in Italy: very high, very long, stone and marble rooms. The actors could not pick up a cue from each other. And what I had to do was to devise a canopy, which had four extendable legs which I brought up and over the action. I also made a rolling baffle, which was 20 or 30 feet high, to reduce the length of the room. So we put that behind the actors. We got rid of a lot of echo by putting bulk into the room. The baffles that I usually use are made out of fiber egg trays. I have these stuck to two pieces of material that are eight feet by four feet; both faces are covered by egg trays that are shielded by chicken wire. And those are brought into the set and used to baffle off extraneous noise or in some cases to deaden the sound in a particularly live room. But this type of solution only works in situations where we are filming rather constrained action.

5
The Doors
Rock 'n' roll on the road

Tod A. Maitland

No novice to the world of film sound, second-genera-tion production mixer Tod A. Maitland, C.A.S, has over 40 pictures under his acetate belt, perhaps half as boom man. In 1990 he received his first Academy Award nomi-nation for **Born on the Fourth of July**, his second gig for Oliver Stone, one of the most successful mainstream di-rectors.

Maitland describes his first meeting in the late '80s with this "crazy, intense director" as terrifying, based mostly on second-hand stories he had heard. In the end the job interview proved straightforward—"one of my easier interviews"—and Maitland decided Stone's repu-tation was largely based on the fact that the director works at a fever pitch, and expects top-notch work from his col-leagues.

Maitland describes Stone's philosophy of recording" as live and as real as possible." Stone, he says, was very interested in **what** sounds his crew could get for him ("ev-erything he wanted"), not **how** they were going to get it.

The Doors took 13 weeks to shoot, a moderate length by any standard, uses 27 of the legendary band's songs, and frequently took on epic proportions in the shooting, employing as it did from 4,000 to 10,000 extras in concert scenes.

Precis

*Working with cinematic realist Oliver Stone from an-
other accomplished production mixer's point of view, use
of earwigs on actors during location music recording,
complex pre-production planning process, and production mixing setup, recording in playback situations,
special production mixes with actors using earwigs.*

Tod A. Maitland's credits

Gloria (1980) John Cassavetes
The Chosen (1981) Jeremy Paul Kagan
Tootsie (1982) Sydney Pollack
Tempest (1982) Paul Mazursky
Off Beat (1986) Michael Dinner
Hannah and Her Sisters (1986) Woody Allen
Radio Days (1987) Woody Allen
3 Men and a Baby (1987) Leonard Nimoy
Suspect (1987) Peter Yates
The Believers (1987) John Schlesinger
Talk Radio (1988) Oliver Stone
The House on Carroll Street (1988) Peter Yates
Cocktail (1988) Roger Donaldson
She-Devil (1989) Susan Seidelman
Cookie (1989) Susan Seidelman
Born on the Fourth of July (1989) Oliver Stone
Jacob's Ladder (1990) Adrian Lyne
One Good Cop (1991) Heywood Gould
JFK (1991) Oliver Stone
The Doors (1991) Oliver Stone

Cape Fear (1991) Martin Scorsese
Night and the City (1992) Irwin Winkler
A Bronx Tale (1993) Robert De Niro
The Age of Innocence (1993) Martin Scorsese
Quiz Show (1994) Robert Redford
Safe Passage (1994) Robert Allan Ackerman
Vanya on 42nd Street (1994) Louis Malle

How did you start the planning process for recording the production track for *The Doors* film?

Once it was decided to go with live vocals, the pre-production team came in and figured out how to do it by coming up with an earwig system. This was the only way to give the actors what they needed and not inhibit their performances. The four band members had earwigs: Val Kilmer played Jim Morrison (vocals), Kyle MacLachlan played Ray Manzarek (keyboard), Kevin Dillon played John Densmore (drums), and Frank Walley played Robby Krieger (guitar). (The centerpiece of the earwigs consisted of the elements out of SONY MDR E 484 earphones).

The pre-production planning team consisted of Mike Minkler, rerecording mixer; Wylie Stateman, supervising sound editor; myself; Paul Rothchild [The Doors record producer]; Keith Klawitter, 24-track engineer, Bud Carr, executive music producer, who does music supervising for all of Oliver's movies, T.J. Omara, my boom man—my eyes and ears of what is going on at camera; and one rep from A-1 Audio, Connie Fernstrom, in charge of all of the earwig mixes.

During six weeks of meetings we worked out these systems: earwigs, speakers, 24-track, how to break down the playback—what we'd be needing to send to each person, how to break down the mixes for everybody, what Oliver needed, what we needed for dailies, how to get

71

Val's live vocals, the drum triggers, and recording all of the live concert sound.

One good thing Oliver [Stone], and Alex Ho [co-producer] do is they keep their crews together—this is our third movie together. Normally the production sound mixer never talks to the sound editors or post production sound mixer, but we talk constantly—from way before the movie starts through production and well into post production. That helped us a lot in the preparation of the movie.

Would you describe how you worked on the set?

During any dialogue scenes and during the concert filming, I was basically coordinating all the dialogue recording. All the dialogue went through my mixing board from which I would send it to the 24-track production master. I would also get feedback from the 24-track and send that out to Oliver and send it out to people who needed to hear things that went on.

Everything went onto the 24-track. We were using two mixing boards. I would mix the dialogue that went to the Le Mobile 24-track and also Val's live singing would go through me and then to the truck. We used Neve preamps beforehand so everything was totally clean.

We only used the 24-track while we were shooting the live performance concerts scenes on about 12 locations. The other times—when we were shooting as if it were a normal movie not a musical—we would shoot 2-track stereo with Dolby SR.

We recorded Val live on the 24-track and we had ambience microphones set up all over the venues.

Also on the 24-track were the live instruments—guitar, keyboard, and the keyboard bass—Val's pre-recorded playback and anywhere from four to six ambience microphones that were strategically placed throughout the audience. This is one of the ways we got some of the best audience tracks you'll ever hear.

The audience tracks were done live with each concert that we filmed. Every time that we rolled the camera these four to six microphones were recording the crowd ambience. And then after filming, we would keep the audience there and have them do yells, so we would get clean individual tracks that we would add in to sweeten up the audience tracks.

Also on the 24-track were individual tracks for each one of my dialogue tracks, because Oliver would mix music and dialogue. In almost all the scenes there's dialogue, even in some of the bigger concerts in between songs, or there are people talking in the audience. For some of these scenes Oliver used multiple cameras; I had a microphone with each camera recording whatever was going on in front of each camera.

Depending on the location we used one of two different types of 24-track units. We started out with an Otari for the smaller venues, such as the Los Angeles Whiskey à Go Go, where all the equipment fit into one room. When we got into larger venues—seconding for Miami Beach, New Haven, The Fillmore—we used Le Mobile, a 24-track mobile truck, run by Guy Charbonneau. Le Mobile had two Studer 24-tracks; the second 24-track could begin rolling automatically in synch with the first 24-track, effectively doubling the running time.

The first day's shooting—the most difficult—probably gives you a good idea of the variety of the challenges we faced during much of the shoot.

The scene starts with them singing "Break on Through to the Other Side." That was a playback situation so each one of the band members needed to have their earwigs in, and we had to have the whole playback situation working.

[In the scene] "Break on Through...." falls apart. The

musicians sit around and talk a little while, then Robby Krieger comes in and says I have this song called "Light My Fire," and he starts strumming it.

We then recorded dialogue, and later the instruments. So we had a playback situation first, then we had a live instrument, live vocals, live dialogue situation. Then as they finally got "Light My Fire" going, they came back and did a second pass at it.

Everything that you could possibly have going at one time we had going.

How did the actors work with the earwigs?

One difficult thing was that [each actor wearing an earwig] had to hear a little bit more of his own instrument, so a monitor mixer had to mix different mixes for each one of them. For instance, Val needed to hear himself in playback because we would pre-record all the songs that would play live in concert. When you see Val very close on camera that's him live. There are other times when his movements on stage really prohibited getting a good live track and those will probably be wider shots. At that point they will go back to Val pre-record. On occasion Val needed to hear himself live, in playback as well as music at a lower level.

There were actually some situations where we could keep the [audience] speakers away enough [from the stage], and Val could hear enough coming through the speakers so that he could do his live singing without a-ffecting the recording we were doing of him. When we didn't give the actors earwigs we would turn up the speakers in the audience and that would give them exactly what they needed [from monitor speakers] on the stage at which point it reverted to a normal playback situation.

Why couldn't you do that all the time?

Since you're doing multiple cameras and multiple takes if Val comes in on a slightly different point in the music and you hear his playback come through his microphone you're going to hear his live voice in his playback over his microphone. And at that point it becomes impossible to separate them. When Val found it very difficult to work with the earwig we would just play the speakers very, very low.

Was Doors music playing on the set during the shooting?

Yes, Oliver wanted to hear Morrison's music throughout the whole movie. While we were recording regular dialogue situations, I would give Oliver the music in his headphones, which he wears all the time. I had all the Doors music on DAT from which I would have a separate mix set up for Oliver. I had marked cue points throughout the Doors music. Those cue points were based on timings that would work with the scene. So Oliver could hear in his headsets the way it was going to work in the final product.

6
Nelson Stoll
Thinking innovatively about production mixing

An Academy Award nominee and 25-year veteran production mixer, Nelson Stoll has more than 30 documentaries, commercials, dramatic shorts, and feature films to his credit.

Precis

Analyzing a shoot for production mixing, TV versus theatrical feature recording, importance of the noise floor, distortion, influence of documentary work, commitment to single microphone use, windscreens, the politics of filmmaking.

Nelson Stoll's credits

Over Under-Sideways Down (1975) Steve Wax
The Last Waltz (1976) Martin Scorsese
Running Fence (1977) David Maysles
        and Albert Maysles
The Grateful Dead (1977) Jerry Garcia
Never Cry Wolf (1982) Carroll Ballard

Dune (1983) David Lynch
Indiana Jones and the Temple of Doom (1984)
    Steven Spielberg
Tai-Pan (1986) Daryl Duke
Total Recall (1991) Paul Verhoeven
Raising Cain (1992) Brian DePalma
Basic Instinct (1992) Paul Verhoeven
Mrs. Doubtfire (1993) Chris Columbus
So I Married an Axe Murderer (1993)
    Thomas Schlamme
Being Human (1994) Bill Forsyth
The Road to Wellville (1994) Alan Parker

Give me an example of how you go about analyzing a shoot for production mixing.

If you take a relatively simple situation such as a master shot of a scene—where the microphone has to be five or six feet overhead—for a scene like this I do a lot of acoustical work to the environment so that the sound is very clear to the microphone or the ear. If you walk into an average kind of living room and you have someone stand in the middle and talk, the sound is very diffuse. It's very hard to hear detail because the sound is bouncing off of all kinds of reflective surfaces. I pay attention to a multitude of small things: attention to acoustics, attention to the directness and simplicity of the chain. I don't like to go through unnecessary amplifiers or unnecessary cables. And the quality of the components is at as high a level as possible, so that the degradation of the sound is minimized as much as possible.

If you take that one example of the overhead microphone in a living room: I've chosen the microphone, the capsule, the kind and length of the cabling, the simplicity of the routing, the acoustical treatment of the room.

All kinds of things that are not revolutionary, they're just acknowledgment and attention to the basics of sound recording and attention to detail.

Is your recording technique different when recording for theatrical versus broadcast television release, such as a TV movie?

Sound has to be compressed for theatrical use because there is a noise floor, which in practice is not the sound of the hiss in the background, it's the sound of the people in the audience, air conditioning, and projector noise.

Every time I record a production track, I have to ask myself: what's this being recorded for? Is this being recorded for TV, where papa's getting up, getting a beer, and the kids are yelling in the background. In other words how low can I let the subtler kinds of sounds go and still have them be heard? Because if I can capture the wealth of low-level detail that's there I've got to turn the level up to bring it above that noise floor. The noise floor is higher for TV than for theaters; the signal to noise ratio is a lot smaller for TV because televisions can't play very loud. I'd say the practical dynamic range for theater is about 60 dB. I don't like to have any low level detail—and that includes the ambience. When I record people inside a room I want to hear not only the people but also whatever else is going on in the room. That has to be heard at a level that's above that noise floor so it can add character to the scene.

I record on a Nagra at 15 ips with Nagramaster—an equalization curve that's part of the stereo Nagra system—which has a signal to noise ratio of 75 dB. The Nagra has a limiter that gives you a 6 dB buffer above that, so, for example, if you're recording a door slam with the high level set at +4 on the meter—which goes to +12—the Nagra will hold that at +4. If it gets above +11 with a sustained sound it goes into gross distortion. But for a short transient like a gunshot, door slam or somebody's yell, I set those levels up higher, the effect of which is to compress the sound at the high end of the spectrum. And that means I can record people at average peak levels around 0 or — 2 or +1, depending on the kind of scene it is. So that for those unexpected peaks that are much higher than that it limits the dynamic range at the top. That's how I compress the dynamic range at the top. And that's a very important kind of limiter for film use.

For TV the dynamic range is about 10 or 15 dB less than it is for theater release.

In practice is that bringing it up from the floor and also down from the top?

Both things.

By about half as much on either end?

Well, no, because when you do the original recording you want to optimize the recording. What that means is you want to have acceptable amounts of distortion. When you do a recording you have two limits: the noise floor at one end and distortion at the other end. I try to record things as hot as they can be—modulating at as high a level as possible—without having distortion. But you can't record everything hot. If there's a scene where people are whispering and later they start yelling at each other you don't want to record the whispers at the same level as the yells, do you? These are the hardest kinds of scenes to record because you have to ask yourself, is this for TV or for theater and how much dynamic range can I get away with?

Why do you tend to integrate new hardware into your film sound work from hi-fi applications rather than more standardized film sound applications?

The hi-fi application is more sophisticated. State- of-the-art sound reproduction usually comes from the highest quality music recording and playback—not theater but professional 2-track stereo playback systems.

My approach towards sound recording originally came out of documentary and very small production where there was no money to replace sound. And usually for documentary sound it's an event that only goes past once, there's not a take two. So I had to very thoroughly understand the abilities of the equipment because you couldn't say [to the director] "That wasn't any good for sound, could we do it again?" The guy's already been shot or the mother already died and the son was already weeping—whatever it was.

How do you prepare differently for a documentary compared to a theatrical feature?

The equipment's a lot simpler on a documentary and that's something else that I tend to do. I like to make things as simple as possible. If there's any way of doing it I like to use one microphone to record a scene. When you do a documentary you are forced to think about what is possible with one microphone: you have to choose that microphone very carefully. You have to especially be cognizant of the implications of putting a microphone in a given position and committing yourself to that position.

In theatrical work many times you use many more microphones for a master shot because you have to, but I strive, if it's at all possible, to be able to use one microphone. That is, to get the sound of whatever's taking place in its multitude of elements so that to the ear it can sound as natural and believable and have as much detail as possible.

What are some examples of modifications you've done to hardware?

Windscreens are an example. When you put a windscreen on a microphone it ideally does two things: it does not stop any of the sound or change the characteristics of the microphone, but it stops the pressure of the wind. That's a pretty hard nut to crack. Every windscreen that's out does neither. So about ten years ago I started listening to all the windscreens that were available and started buying raw materials and making microphone suspensions and windscreens. I use Schoeps microphones, which I consider the best-sounding condenser microphones available; they're the most natural-sounding ones. The windscreeens that they made sound really bad. And this was before I had strong engineering skills to be able to verify what I heard.

In addition to the two characteristics I just mentioned another that I consider in designing windscreens is cavity resonance. The first one I made was a large windscreen, one usable in winds over 30 mph., which is essentially the one I use today. Its design takes into account cavity resonance, the polar response of the microphone, the outside surface and the way the wind sounds when it hits that surface, the high-frequency attenuation, and the physical structure in terms of the mechanical resonance.

What modifications have you made to the Nagra's in-line filters?

These Schoeps microphones have incredible bass response.

Too much?

Yes. They're perfect for the lowest note of an organ, they're very flat down there and sometimes that's desirable. But usually you're recording dialogue and the male voice only really goes down to the fundamentals to around 125 Hz. and you can lose a little bit of the chest cavity on a very large man, and you really want to record down to about 100 Hz. But anything below that you don't want to record because what you're getting is mechanical problems through handling noise and the wind impacting the diaphragm. So you want a bandwidth limit on the low end of the spectrum. Because some of the Nagra's built-in filters are not as useful as others, I modified the less useful ones to take care of this problem.

On the Nagra 4.2 rotary switch, the HP2 (High PassNumber 2) was so high that it castrates all but the squeakiest of female voices, anything that has anything of low end power to it. So I shifted it down just enough to where it was acceptable: from around 150 Hz., now it's down to about 115.

What are the most challenging aspects of your work?

The biggest challenges I face involve the politics of filmmaking: trying to find the space, time and energy to discuss what is possible to get out of production sound considering the time and financial constraints that exist in every project. The hardest challenges are not the technical challenges, those are relatively simple and relatively straight forward if you know who to ask.

Take a worst case example: say you go onto a commercial that's only going to be a three-day job and half an hour before you're to start shooting they show you the story boards. You're trying to find out what they want and expect, what is possible to give them and how you might alter their expectations—present them with alternatives—efficiently and quickly.

In general how do you think the quality of film sound could be improved?

If everyone who works with film audio were to have a thorough understanding of sound basics—from the original concept of the film right to the final reproduction in the theater—this would greatly enhance film sound quality. Most of the time it's such a fragmented process and there's so little communication between all the diverse elements of the process that the sound gets castrated each time it's transferred. So that what you end up with even if the sound is recorded very, very well initially is a sound that is not preserved carefully all the way through.

SECTION TWO

POST PRODUCTION SOUND

7
Amadeus
Academy Award-winning post production

Mark Berger
(part one)

On the occasion of this interview in 1984 the atmosphere at the Saul Zaentz Film Center in Northern California was quite heady. The previous fall the much-awaited $15-million production of **Amadeus**, directed by Milos Forman, had headquartered itself here after many months of shooting in authentic Central European locations. Earlier in the year Academy Award nominations poured into the full service post production facility for two films, **Never Cry Wolf** and **The Right Stuff**. The culmination came when **The Right Stuff** won that year's Academy Award for Best Sound.

Although the Zaentz Center continues to be one of the best-outfitted West coast post production facilities, its reputation must be largely attributable to its freelance craftsmen. Chief among these is the three-time Academy Award-winning sound mixer Mark Berger [**Apocalypse Now** (1979), **The Right Stuff** (1983), **Amadeus** (1984)].

As is so often the case in this industry, Berger did not come fully hatched from some great sound mixing school in the great beyond. Instead, his work in sound finds its origins in a youthful interest in (and many years' playing) trombone and a healthy dose (mostly self-administered) of college classical music appreciation courses. He capped this pre-professional period by working four years in radio documentaries at the University of California's

Radio Television Theater, where he helped produce two half-hour documentaries a week. In retrospect, his next job seems to have been the perfect transition for Berger into his sound career: the often innovative world of public television documentaries at KQED-TV, San Francisco. As with so many skilled film craftsmen in the San Francisco area, Mark Berger's career got a considerable boost from Francis Coppola's filmmaking there in the '70s on pictures such as **Godfather II** (1972) and **Apocalypse Now** (1979).

This very accomplished sound mixer attributes his success not only to a life-long pursuit of what interests him most, but also to something he had no control over: his genes. As Berger describes it, his ability to concentrate on and remember endless details of the complex sound mixing process on little or no sleep—in a word, his physical constitution—accounts for his success as much as years of work at his craft. For instance, during the last few months of sound work on **Amadeus**, weeks would go by without a day off or less than a 15-hour work day (that's 9 a.m. to midnight!). Through it all, Berger says, he is able to maintain a high level of ear/hand coordination ("...you hear something and you react to it....") on little or no sleep.

Precis

*Director Milos Forman's requirements for his sound tracks—focused sound aesthetic compared to his filming aesthetic, Francis Coppola's approach to same, how these differing approaches affect Berger's aesthetic, elements Berger was given to work with on **Amadeus**, John Strauss' work as music editor, Foley, the effect of* *home stereo systems on theatrical movie sound tracks, mixing early TV documentaries compared to **Amadeus**.*

Mark Berger's credits

Godfather II (1972) Francis Coppola
One Flew Over the Cuckoo's Nest (1974)
 Milos Forman
Invasion of the Body Snatchers (1977) Phil Kaufman
Apocalypse Now ** (1979) Francis Coppola
No Nukes (1979) Julian Schlossberg,
 Danny Goldberg, Anthony Potenza
Dragonslayer (1981) Matthew Robbins
The Plague Dogs (1982) Martin Rosen
The Right Stuff ** (1983) Phil Kaufman
Amadeus ** (1984) Milos Forman
Heaven Help Us (1985) Michael Dinner
Kiss of the Spider Woman (1985) Hector Babenco
The Legend of Bill Jean (1985) Matthew Robbins
Smooth Talk (1985) Joyce Chopra
That Was Then, This is Now (1985)
 Christopher Cain
April Fool's Day (1986) Fred Walton
Blue Velvet (1986) David Lynch
The Mosquito Coast (1986) Peter Weir
River's Edge (1986) Tim Hunter
Dear America (1987) Bill Couturie
Ernest Goes to Camp (1987) John Cherry
Gaby—A True Story (1987) Luis Mandoki
Stacking (1987) Martin Rosen
Break of Dawn (1988) Isaac Artenstein
The Chocolate War (1988) Keith Gordon
Dirty Rotten Scoundrels (1988) Frank Oz
Ernest Saves Christmas (1988) John Cherry

My Best Friend is a Vampire (1988) Jimmy Huston
The Unbearable Lightness of Being (1988)
    Phil Kaufman
The Wizard of Loneliness (1988) Jenny Bowen
Checking Out (1989) David Leland
Winter People (1989) Ted Kotcheff
Cadillac Man (1990) Roger Donaldson
Common Threads: Stories from the Quilt (1990)
    Robert Epstein, Jeffrey Friedman
Ernest Goes to Jail (1990) John Cherry
The Guardian (1990) William Friedkin
Madhouse (1990) Tom Ropelawski
Mermaids (1990) Richard Benjamin
State of Grace (1990) Phil Joanou
At Play in the Fields of the Lord (1991)
    Hector Babenco
Closetland (1991) Radha Bharadwaj
Crooked Hearts (1991) Michael Bortman
Mortal Thoughts (1991) Alan Rudolph
Folks: A Midnight Clear! (1992) Ted Kotcheff
Dragon: The Bruce Lee Story (1993) Rob Cohen
Equinox (1993) Alan Rudolph
Mr. Wonderful (1993) Anthony Minghella
Money for Nothing (1993) Ramon Menendez
Motorama (1993) Barry Shils
Mrs. Parker and the Vicious Circle (1994)
    Alan Rudolf
Serial Mom (1994) John Waters
Squanto: A Warrior's Tale (1994) Xavier Koller

Would you describe your job on *Amadeus*?

My job on **Amadeus** was basically to be responsible for the way the final sound track sounds and how it relates to the picture, which involves mixing the sound.

A lot of people in the audience are aware of picture editing in that they know that the picture's been manipulated, that the sets have been manipulated and that various cuts are artificially made to create a particular effect. People are even demanding that now in terms of more special effects and more flashy visual things. So, there's a lot of visual sophistication in what people see on the screen.

But along with that, people still are very naive about what they hear in that they subconsciously expect that what they hear is what it really sounded like when the picture was shot, with the obvious exception of things like the space movies and **Star Wars**, when you're in outer space and it's obviously special effects and created. But in realistic dramas people don't bring to the sound track the same critical faculties and sophistication they do to the picture. But actually the soundtrack is just as highly manipulated and just as artificial and just as contrived as any picture cut.

So, my job is to take all these sound elements that go into a track—which is usually broken up into dialogue and music and the sound effects, which are added later— and mix them and blend them in such a way that it seems perfectly natural, doesn't call attention to itself as apart from the picture but yet creates whatever desired effect we're after. So, if our work in creating the sound is invisible and doesn't draw attention to itself then it's successful. If it starts to draw attention to itself then we're not doing so well.

At the start of this project what were the guidelines and elements that you were given to work with?

Well, I have worked with Milos [Forman] before [as sound mixer on **One Flew Over the Cuckoo's Nest**], so I knew that the dialogue he basically likes to hear is exactly what was recorded at the time of filming without any special effects. He's very much after just the straight realistic presentation of what goes on, as opposed to adding in a lot of background voices, creating things happening off-screen in the room, when you're inside Mozart's apartment and there's street noise going on outside, but we don't hear the street because we're really not interested in it. Even though we've just been outside and had seen a very active street scene with jugglers and dancing bears and yellers, when we go into the apartment all that disappears. Milos doesn't want to hear it because that's not part of the drama; the drama's happening inside the room.

That distinction is not clear to me.

Well, as director you have a choice: you can either continue the street sounds as you would hear them inside Mozart's apartment through the windows, so that the following scenes play with the street sounds in the background, or you could just drop the street sounds completely and play the scene entirely as though it were nowhere and there was nothing at all happening outside. His choice was that he didn't want any sense of what we've just seen once the film moves inside.

And that's a purely stylistic approach. When we're in a dialogue scene and we're focusing on the dialogue and the interaction between two principal characters, he's not interested in any sort of background sound that refers to anything that's gone on previously or might be going on outside.

Do you see that as relating to a larger aesthetic that he has which relates to other ways he treats sound?

It's a very focused aesthetic and some people could

say it's a rather two-dimensional aesthetic in that what you see on the screen is all you hear. And it's very specifically used to create a contrast between cuts, that he really is only interested in going one layer deep and what you see is what you hear. But his filming is like that, too, in that in the dialogue scenes the costumes are very rich and very wonderful but the action is generally focused only between two people at once. It's a very focused approach so you only pay attention to what the people are saying.

Can you contrast that with any other director you've worked with?

Take Francis Coppola on **Apocalypse Now** [Berger was a sound mixer]. In the scene when they're landing on the beach to go surfing, Francis will have 47 different things happening in the frame at the same time. It's like reading the old MAD Magazine where there's the main action on screen and then in the middle foreground there'll be another action. In the background there'll be 14 other things happening. So, everytime you see the movie, you look in a different part of the frame and there's something you didn't notice before.

Well in the same way, we can develop the sound for each one of those layers. So, you have the foreground action that's happening, then in the background there'll be people marching and a couple of helicopters landing and there'll be some guy yelling at somebody else, and somebody's digging a trench and there's a shell coming in. So you have many more layers of sound. A very different approach.

Did you have to make a major mental transition working with Forman after working with a director such as Coppola? How does it affect the way you work?

93

No, it doesn't involve a major shift. It's as if I said: "You know I'm going to paint this picture blue so use blue paint. I'm going to paint this picture red and I'll use red paint." But what you're doing is you're still painting a picture. You're always keeping in mind the director's particular philosophy. If it comes down to a question of "What can we do to make this scene sound more interesting?," with Francis you could think of 14 different ways of creating interesting background—something that's happening off-screen. With Milos the answer is: nothing. He says: "Just keep the dialogue clean and understandable."

Would it be fair to say, therefore, that your work on something like *Amadeus* is more technically oriented—involves less of your creative imagination—than on something like *Apocalypse Now*?

Well, there's certainly a lot more room for creative expression on something like **Apocalypse Now** than there is on **Amadeus**, where we were more concerned with maintaining the subtlety of performance that exists, in no way compromising any of the expressiveness of the actors or any of the subtleties of the performances.

Can you tell me what you were given to work with at the outset of your work on *Amadeus*?

We had the original quarter-inch tapes of dialogue that were recorded on location, the 24-track tapes of the music that had been recorded (with Neville Marriner), and there were also guide tracks that had been made from the music that were used when they would play the music on the set while they were filming and the actors would pretend as though they were hearing the music as it would later be put in the film. For example, all the operas, all the musical numbers, were done to playback. It's like the old **American Bandstand** where somebody would get up and mouth the words but what you really heard was a record.

Did Milos give you any guidelines regarding how the music was going to be cut?

The person who did all of the music cutting and editing was John Strauss, who'd worked with him on **Hair** and **Ragtime**, but Milos was the one who would cut the music. When they cut the picture, they cut the picture and the music together. So, what we get is a guide track that has the music on it where they want it and the dialogue where they want it and any special effects that they have where they want it.

So, in the beginning we would be doing these scratch mixes where he would say: "All right, reel 13 is ready." We'd go downstairs, he'd play it, he'd play the music that he'd cut, and he'd play the dialogue. And he'd say: "Now here I want knocks on the door: here, here and here. And then I want to have very, very quiet footsteps and the music has to be very loud. And then on this cut the music goes down and we should hear his voice very clearly saying this." And then we'd go upstairs and we'd do these scratch mixes which later became the guides for people to work on during the final mix. And then as the picture changed, each time there was a picture change we had a screening, we had to do a new scratch mix [cf. Berger **Mosquito Coast** discussion of temp mixes below]. So, it was constant evolution of the effects and the music and the dialogue.

It's not clear to me what John Strauss did.

Strauss was the music editor. He took care of all the music, he made all the music cuts. He determined how pieces of music would go together. He made suggestions for cutting to the director. And he sat with me and we did all the mix-downs from 24-track together. And he was basically responsible for the musical quality of the film. For example, the music is edited: you have a piano concerto that runs ten minutes when only three minutes of it is used in the film, the beginning section, the end section, and maybe a middle section. So, somebody has to make those cuts.

Did you have a lot more hardware to work with this time than on *Cuckoo's Nest?*

Oh, yeah, but that was about ten years ago, before Dolby stereo. We had a completely different studio. **Cuckoo's Nest** was done mono, at Fantasy but at Studio "A." **Amadeus** we're doing 70 mm. stereo opticals and monos, and we've got a much larger board. We're using 24-track [Ampex] at the same time we're using film locked up together. Instead of recording onto just three tracks of a master, we're recording onto 12 tracks—two 6-track 35 mm. full coat recorders—to keep the dialogue, the music and the effects all separate so we can make changes. [Berger noted that six tracks is the greatest number of audio tracks that could be recorded at that time on 35 mm. full coat].

How are you using the 24-track machine?

We use it as playback, not for recording masters onto. For example, we have a 24-track that has nothing but applause on it. So there's maybe a hundred kinds of applause—start, stop—of all lengths, of all intensities, of all numbers of people. And if we need an applause, say, in the middle of "The Magic Flute," the "Queen of the Night" aria, and the one that the editors have cut for us isn't very good, we'll put up the 24-track and lock it up and just take it off the 24-track directly onto the master. But you can't start and stop recording on a 24-track the way we can on film, so we don't use it for mastering. Plus the whole industry is set up to work on film.

Can you see any disadvantages in working on film versus 24-track audio?

No. The advantage in working on film is that the whole industry is set up to do it all the way down the line; because it has to go out of our studios into the real world at some point to be made into 70 mm. and optical. Making changes is a lot easier because you can edit the film to correspond to the picture changes where you can't do that with 24-track. You can move individual elements around a lot more, like if you've got four tracks of dialogue and three tracks of music and you want to advance the music a frame or two to change the synch slightly, you just advance the music a frame or two. If it's all on 24-track you can't do that because everything's locked together.

How many 6-track machines do you have available at Fantasy?

Seven or eight [at the time of this interview—np] But those are used for masters. See, the individual elements before they have been mixed on are single-track or three-track. There's 18 of those machines.

Who assembled the applause tracks on the 24-tracks?

97

We went out and recorded them. Dave Parker took them off of our Nagra and laid them onto the 24-track. We recorded stuff at Hertz Hall [University of California], we went to KQED-FM and got some of their recordings of performances at Davies Hall and Herbst Theater; we took the applause sections out of that.

How did you distinguish between them?

You know: "Davies 40 seconds, mild," "Davies 20 seconds, intense," "Davies 35 seconds, polite." They also have numbers like DP 406-2, a card catalogue numbering system.

Do you have any anecdotes you would like to tell about the mixing of *Amadeus*?

There's one scene where Mozart indicates his disdain for another composer (Salieri) by replacing a piano cadence at the end of a piece that he's playing with a rather loud passing of wind from severe flatulence. It was a subject of a lot of fun to (a) record the effect and (b) to try to guess whose it was and (c) whether or not it was actually real or just blowing on your arm or something. To this day we don't really know where the effect that we used came from or who made it or how it was made.

But it was made in this building?

Well, we're not even sure of that because various people took the tape recorders home for various periods of time. And certain restaurants were called upon to provide...well, we would go out to restaurants and have certain meals with the idea that we'd come back and record a lot of effects.

What other effects were recorded here at Fantasy?

Foley was done to video in another studio. Foley is all of the movement and the footsteps. That runs the length of the film because from the very first reel when people are walking up the stairs, to the end of the film as Salieri's being wheeled off in his wheelchair, there are background movement effects. Every scene will have something in it, even where there's just a close-up of Salieri in his wheelchair talking to us. Whenever he moves there's the sound of silk or linen or a creak of his wheelchair that has to be added in.

When was that done?

As they're cutting the picture we're doing that. Before we get to the final mix. [Berger pointed out that all of Foley took three weeks to do].

Would you comment on how changes in technology have affected your work as a sound mixer?

Mostly it's the change from Academy mono, which is one speaker with a very limited frequency response. It's like the difference between 78s and LPs in stereo.

One system is a single channel with limited frequency response and the other is four channels—in the case of Dolby stereo—or six channels—in the case of 70 mm. It just gives you more variables to work with, more room to move around in. Even though the sounds that you put in may be the same, they're highlighted a lot more and they become a more enveloping experience. So while there's more parameters to work with, more variables to control, there's also more space to move around in.

Given the same sounds, in the days before Dolby all you had was basically how you mixed it: loud, soft, bass, treble, stuff like that. When Dolby came along with their 4-track stereo optical all of a sudden you add now left, center, right, and surround. (One of the first Dolby stereo features was **Nashville** around 1975.) And the frequency response has opened up to match a lot closer the home recordings.

Of course, 70 mm. always existed, which was and still is the highest-fidelity format around. But those pictures were pretty limited before because they were very expensive. They were limited mostly to roadshow musicals like **Oklahoma** and **South Pacific**. The vast majority of films that people went to see were strictly mono.

What brought the expense down?

I think when Dolby started on their stereo optical, along with that went an increase in attention people paid to sound, which made it more feasible for people to release more in 70 mm. Also the fact that before it was limited mostly to musicals but now every large budget film that has a lot of sound effects in it wants to get a 70 release because it's a big show-piece thing and they can charge a lot of money for it and people like to see it.

Basically the technical changes meant you have a larger canvas to paint on and you have more brushes. The canvas is the speaker system behind the screen, the four tracks of sound: left, center, right, and surround; instead of being a small canvas that sits in the middle of the theater, now wraps all the way around you, because you've got the surround speakers and the left, center, and right. So now you can do things in true stereo more like what people are used to hearing at home.

Things had gotten to the point where everybody's home stereo was better than the best theater, so people got used to hearing very high quality sound. So the theaters did something to catch up. And that was the appeal of the stereo. It's gotten to the point now where the name "Dolby Stereo" to a lot of people means "loud," in some ways. And people want to hear things coming from behind them or they want to feel that there's stuff going on all around them. That's sort of a degradation of what it's really about, but those are the marketing appeals of it.

If you had to single out one piece of hardware that's made your job easier since you worked on *Cuckoo's Nest* what would that be?

The biggest single advance was the ability to punch in and out of recording without hearing where you started and stopped recording. Before they had punch-in and punch-out you used to have to mix live all the cues, all the changes. Everything had to be done as you were going because if you made a mistake that was it. You blew it. You had to go back and start all over again. When I was working at KQED [TV PBS/San Francisco] doing 16 mm. documentaries, we'd mix in half-hour reels. And it's a lot to remember a half-hour's worth of changes. So we used to write out very elaborate cue sheets and we'd try to confine it to like three and four, five tracks at most.

We'd have all sorts of people at the consoles whose only job was to change certain controls at certain times. We'd get editors and assistants and gofers and everybody in there. And we'd say: "All right, at 300 feet you take this and you turn it back to there." And so we'd do hours and hours and hours of rehearsals trying to get it down. And then we'd say: "Everybody take a deep breath. Let's go." And we'd start and try to make it all the way through the reel without blowing it. And if somebody did make a mistake you either had to accept it or start over again, or maybe find a place where you could stop and make a splice but that was sort of hard to do.

And when they got this punch-in, punch-out recording all that went away. You could work on very short sections. If you made a mistake you just went back and matched your levels to where you had been before and hit the record button and it started to record. You didn't hear the machine start to record. It just kept on going and it was very smooth. And the same for stopping to record. You didn't then have to go all the way to the end of the reel.

7
The Mosquito Coast
in post production

Mark Berger
(part two)

This interview was conducted toward the completion of editing on **The Mosquito Coast**. I was allowed to watch a mixing session during one of the final days of work at the Fantasy Studios. The session was conducted in the mixing theater, a moderate-sized fifty-odd-seat auditorium at the extremities of which are a full-sized cinemascope screen and a mixing board seating about five or six. The commanding view from this mixing board makes one feel like Captain Nemo aboard the mythical Nautilus.

When I arrived Berger was occupying the Nemo seat, while a somewhat athletic and youthful-looking fellow was sitting where I had never seen anyone sit before on the three or four steps that separate the mixing board area from the auditorium below. (Some years before I watched rerecording of **Amadeus,** resulting in the preceding Berger interview, Chapter 7, part one). During the following hour this figure moved about restlessly, sometimes sitting next to Berger at the multi-colored mixing board, sometimes slumping alone, in one of the theater's back row seats. This figure was the director of **The Mosquito Coast**, the Australian Peter Weir.

Berger was calm, cool, and businesslike as he moved briskly through the session, speaking frequently into the intercom to the projectionist behind and above, repeatedly asking him to project sections of film and sound, and talking easily with Weir. This is what he does for hundreds upon hundreds of hours a year at Fantasy. And has done ever since he became one of the studio's main Supervising Re-Recording Mixers years ago.

The story of **The Mosquito Coast** (the movie) began in 1982, six months after publication of the acclaimed Paul Theroux novel, when a producer named Jerome Hellman purchased the movie rights with his own money, giving Theroux $250,000 plus five percent of the profits. The iconoclast, Hellman—whose previous credits included **Midnight Cowboy, Day of the Locust**, and **Coming Home**—said he saw a lot of himself in Theroux's character of Allie Fox, the somewhat eccentric Massachusetts inventor who uproots himself and his family out of disgust with the American way of life and searches for a new identity in the dense jungle of Central America.

Fresh from the international success of **The Year of Living Dangerously**, Peter Weir agreed to direct **The Mosquito Coast**. It was to have been his first American picture. But when Hellman's original financing through Warner Bros. dissolved when that company had a major change of management, Weir moved on to direct Harrison Ford in **Witness**.

Finally, early in 1985, Saul Zaentz announced that he would finance the $16-million production. Shooting began in February, 1986, in Belize, and lasted 17 weeks with two additional weeks in Georgia [cf. Chris Newman interview about the production mixing for this picture, Chapter 1, part two]. Immediately after shooting was completed, Weir and editor Thom Noble worked for 10 weeks in Australia assembling a three-and-a-half hour rough cut of the picture. During mid-summer of '86 **The Mosquito Coast** moved to the Zaentz Fantasy Studios for the enormously intricate tasks of arriving at a fine picture cut, and editing and mixing the myriad layers of sound to form the final track of the two-hour feature film. (Before setting to work in Berkeley, Peter Weir also worked for a short period in Los Angeles with composer, Maurice Jarre preparing a music score.)

Generally speaking the line of command in the complex process of making a motion picture—starting with the all-important matter of financing—goes from the executive producer on **The Mosquito Coast**, Saul Zaentz, through the line producer (Jerome Hellman) to director (Peter Weir), who works very closely in the shooting situation with the cinematographer (John Seale). In post production—after all the film has been shot—the primary creative team generally consists of the director, the film editor (in this case Thom Noble) the supervising sound editor (Alan Splet), the supervising rerecording mixer (Mark Berger), and a post production sound crew of perhaps ten highly skilled sound editors and their assistants.

Precis

The job of supervising rerecording mixer on **The Mosquito Coast** *defined, temp mix, pre-mix, director Peter Weir's approach to mixing, special location mixing problems—the wind, the music mix, examples of gutsy music cues, compared to the music of Charles Ives, the occasion for picture editor Thom Noble to cut music, relationship to the mix, Fantasy Studios methods versus Hollywood's, aesthetic of sound editing versus picture editing, when is the decision to loop made, manifold ways sound functions in a movie, technical versus non-technical aspects of mixing process, reading the director's mind, the process not the result, what Berger*

105

enjoys the least, salvaging production track versus looping (ADR), Weir's role.

What does it mean to be a supervising re-recording mixer on a picture like *The Mosquito Coast*?

I'm like the chef in a restaurant who takes all the ingredients which are prepared by the other chefs and blends them together into the final cooked product, and arranges it on the plate so that it's presented well, and everything tastes just right so you don't taste too much pepper or too much salt, so that it all blends together into a whole meal that people enjoy as an entity.

We take all the sound elements that have been prepared by the editors and, working with the director, we mix them all together so that it accentuates the action and preserves the character of the performances and emphasizes certain cuts. Our work enhances the emotional and narrative flow of a picture so that the entire sound track of the picture appears to be a seamless work that people don't really pay a whole lot of attention to, per se, but that exerts a very powerful influence on how the movie plays.

How did the process of sound mixing on *The Mosquito Coast* begin?

First of all I saw the rough cut of the film several times. Then I talked with Thom Noble [the picture editor], Peter [Weir, the director], Alan Splet, the supervising sound editor, and the dialogue editors.

What were the conversations about?

About how we're going to handle this or that scene: Is it going to be looped dialogue? Is it going to be production dialogue? How many voices are going to be in the background? Are there going to be heavy effects or just simple effects?

Now, do they know the answers to all these questions?

Sometimes they do. Other times they'll say, "Well, I don't know. We'll just have to try it and see. Let's prepare it both ways, or let's leave that decision for later."

So then comes the first day of dialogue mixing, which is where we start. The dialogue editors have been working for three or four weeks to prepare these reels.

Before dialogue editing began on *The Mosquito Coast*, how long were you working on the picture?

Maybe two weeks, during which time I was doing temp mixes. This involved smoothing out different cuts, trying different dialogue lines, trying different narrations, trying scenes with music, without music. If you take away the music then you've got to have something there, so you put in some effects. We tried different effects to see what Peter liked; we spent a lot of time getting just the right sound for the wind chimes, for instance.

Give me a definition of a temp mix.

A temp mix is an approximation of what the final mix is going to be like. All the elements are not necessarily as fine-tuned as they would be later, but it's something that you do fairly quickly, in a day or two, with some music in, with all the dialogue that wants to be there, with some of the most important effects that make it different. Its

107

purpose is to give you an idea of whether or not the picture will play with all the elements in place. It's also something that's easily changed, so you can see what works, make changes and try it again. The music may not be the music that was written, it may be music off of records, or music from other films, that's the right mood and the right length.

Did you know what to put in those temp mixes from discussions with Weir?

Yes. Or you say, "Peter come listen to this." At this point he is spending most of his time editing the picture, but he'll come up and listen to the temp mix, and say, "Well, yeah, I don't like the wooden sound in the chimes. See if you can go more for the seashell kind of clinky stuff."

How would you define a pre-mix?

On a bigger film you break things down into separate areas: dialogue is considered one area, so certain people just edit the dialogue. There may be ten or fifteen tracks of just dialogue that you have to combine so that everything is smooth—all of the [sound] perspectives match the camera angles and the best takes are taken for each actor. A sentence may be made up of three or four different takes; it may involve some lines that were added in the studio. So all of this has to be mixed together and smoothed out so it all sounds like somebody is saying it at the time it's being filmed. In order to do that you'll take just the dialogue and mix it down to a 6-track recording that's blended and equalized, so that if you just play the dialogue by itself, everything would be smooth.

But that's just one element; next you have to add in the sound effects and the music. So the process of smoothing out the dialogue and mixing it to make it sound right is called the dialogue pre-mix, because it comes before the main mix, which is where everything [dialogue, music, effects] is put together.

How was Peter Weir to work with?

Peter Weir is, perhaps, one of the best persons in the world to work with: he's very open and warm. He has a receptivity to ideas and creates a feeling of everybody working as a unit. He was totally appreciative and blown away by the kind of work that people were doing up here; he's just not used to it.

Peter Weir used to be an actor, so he does amazing things with his voice, so whenever we needed a voice for anything—it could have been any character—Peter would go up to the microphone and say "Oh, I'll do it, I'll do it! Just record it and put it in." And then he'd speak and whatever came out was perfect. So in the film he talks in some kind of Creole-pidgin dialect for the farmworkers who are cutting the asparagus. He's this character, Francis Lumley, saying, "Move it over there, put it down," when they're carrying the ice. He's Harrison Ford saying, "I'm sorry, I'm sorry!" after he's thrown Mother down. He's the voice of a cartoon character on a TV show when the Reverend and his family are watching television. He's some boy whistling a tune when the workers are building [the fictional jungle settlement of] Jeronimo. His voice in all its various disguises is in about a dozen different places in the film and they're all wonderful.

Did Weir initially set up any guidelines or standards for the sound mixing of *Mosquito Coast*?

They sort of developed as we went along. We would do a dialogue pre-mix and then he would come up and listen to it. From working back and forth with this, we got a feel for the ways he liked to play things: how rich a texture he wanted, how many things he wanted to have happening at once, how he liked to play perspective changes. And it was the same with the effects pre-mixing.

Peter's the kind of guy who knows what he wants but will listen to whatever it is you've done, and then will tell you how he wants things changed, and then knows when he's got it. He's the perfect kind of person to work for because he's not so dogmatic that [he would say] "You have to do it this way."

Once, for example, I was going along playing a section of dialogue for him, and I missed a cue and turned on somebody's line about three words too late. Harrison was supposed to be saying, "Not now Mother, we'll do it when we get there." But I missed it and then I realized "Oops! Something's supposed to be happening," and I opened up [the volume level] and we heard, "...We'll do it when we get there." I said "Sorry Peter, I missed that." But he said, "No, no, no, that was interesting. I liked it. I liked it without the line. Maybe we don't really need that line. Let's try it again—only this time leave out the whole line." So we played it again and we left out the whole line. Then he said, "Just take the second half of the line, the way you did the first time." So I went back and did it.

So what should have been a mistake turned into something that he really liked, that he grabbed onto instantly and became part of the way the film was mixed. That happened quite frequently—not that I made a lot of mistakes, you understand, but just in the course of playing things, where you don't think you're doing anything, he would always be there listening.

Were there occasions when Weir was critical of the way you worked?

No, he would not be critical of the way you did it, personally. It would be an evaluation of what worked in the film. He would never say anything like, "Hah, you really blew that one!" or "That was terrible. I didn't like the way you did it." He would say: "That's was interesting. I'm not sure we should have the insects so loud. Let's try it a little softer this time." Or he might say, "Wow, I never really heard it with those sounds in there so loud before, where it's fighting the dialogue. That's kind of interesting because this is struggling against nature, and maybe we should have to listen to him over the roar of the insects a bit." So it was never anything personal that you had done, it was what had happened to the sound going into the film.

He would never say something like, "I don't like that"?

Yeah, sure. He'd say, "No, no, no, that doesn't work at all, I don't like that. Do it the other way." But you could also say to him, "Gee, Peter, this isn't working for me. I think the music shouldn't be so ethereal up to the part where we get to the church because it's not paying off properly." And he'd say, "Hum, all right let's try it that way." Then we'd play it, and he'd either say, "Yeah, that's right, let's do it that way," or he'd say, "Yeah, I see your point but that doesn't work here for me because we want them to be ethereal until they get there."

Can you compare Weir's way of working with other directors you've worked with?

I'll compare it to the way I worked with Francis [Coppola], who basically wasn't there. Francis would come in when the mix was done and listen to it and make

111

his suggestions for how things were working, but that was because he had worked with Walter [Murch] for so long; he left the sound for Walter to do the way he wanted.

Was this the first time you've worked with an Australian director?

There's nothing particularly special about Australians. Well, there is: he's "one of the guys." He'd come in at five o'clock with a beer in his hand and say, "What's going on here? If this were Australia, everybody would be sitting around with a beer in their hand." To which our response would be, "That's great Peter. Here, have another beer, but somebody's got to stay awake." He was very accessible and that was a very pleasant surprise.

The Mosquito Coast was shot almost entirely in exteriors: did this pose any special problems for you as a re-recording mixer?

Well, there's a thing that happens if there's a very light breeze: the palm trees and all the foliage will start to rustle. It makes a sound that's like sitting next to an air conditioner, but it's not identifiable as wind because you don't see anything moving and it doesn't change...there are no audible gusts and puffs and blusters and stuff. So, it's just sort of sitting there like this air conditioner noise. So you deal with it.

How?

We pick another take that was shot at a different time—you add some wind so that there's a little bit of something else happening. Or we sprinkle a little mixer dust on it and say a few incantations and the noise will mysteriously go away. We have our noise reduction techniques: filters and equalization. It's a balancing act: you want to take away as much of the noise as possible but you want to change the dialogue as little as possible. The ear will accept sound a lot easier if it's constant than if it comes and goes a lot. If you use a lot of filters and noise gates, things tend to come and go. So we try to clean the sound up as much as possible and then we try to establish the sound in the beginning by having the wind blow hard, for example. And then, once the wind blows, you take it away a little bit—you drop it down. Once having established the wind, having it constant throughout the rest of the scene isn't very noticeable. That's the way it works: if you have an obnoxious sound, you can establish it loud at the beginning, then take it away, down to the level of where it persists throughout the dialogue and it almost becomes invisible.

There wasn't much music in *The Mosquito Coast*, was there?

There was very little. There are perhaps three main cues in the entire film: the opening music, the trip up the river and the closing music. For this two-hour film there was less than 25 minutes of scored music.

That's another interesting thing about Peter: for all of the screenings that we had and the few temp mixes that we did, it seemed that every time we did something he would take out another music cue. In the beginning, when they began cutting it, there was music all over the place. And then as the story began to emerge and as the power of the performances began to become more and more focused, the music became more and more superfluous, so he would just take it out. I've never seen a director take out so much music.

It's really gutsy what Weir does with music. There are scenes where any other director would have put music,

113

and where even the audience will think to themselves, "Where's the music?" Two places in particular: where Harrison and his family are standing in front of Fat Boy [the itinerant inventor's most massive invention] before they light it up for the first time. One of the kids is taking a picture and there's a medium [shot] pan[ning] across to Harrison and the family standing there. There's absolutely nothing happening on the sound track; there's a little bit of background noise in the jungle. Nothing for a good thirty seconds, which would have been a perfect place emotionally and soundwise for music. No music.

And then there's the very final scene after Harrison has been shot and they've escaped from Gurney's Mission and they're in the belly of the whale—in this skeleton of a boat—floating down the river. Any other filmmaker would have had a music cue there. In fact one was written for it. But Peter felt that given what was coming and for what we'd been through, the scene didn't need music. So all we hear is the sound of the jungle and some wind chimes that are on the boat. And because it's so quiet and because there's no music, the scene has an intensified reality that's very powerful. It almost seems like a documentary.

Where you would expect music there's none and where he does use music he didn't use just one cue, he used maybe two and three cues on top of each other: two entirely different pieces of music playing at once. It's a lot like Charles Ives. So when Allie and the family are in Mosquitia, for instance, there's this great soca music cue, kind of a Reggae cue called "Give Me Soca," that plays as half source, half scored. As the soca music is playing, we see these girls coming out on a boat; they're singing a song about Jesus. And then when they land on the dock these same girls are also singing another song about Jesus, all the while this soca music is playing. So we have this cacophony of voices, of music, another kind of music, all happening at once.

Had you ever layered music in the manner of a Charles Ives composition before in mixing a film score?

Not to this extent. I can't think of a time when there were two pieces of music both playing full out that are so completely different.

And how did that come about on this picture?

It was in their [Noble's and Weir's] idea of the cut. It started out with just the synch of the girls singing on the boat as they come into shore, but then they decided that the whole scene needed some music to carry it all the way through. So they started the scored soca music earlier and it didn't quite work right. At one point they dropped out the music of the girls singing in the boat, but that didn't work either. So they started the music of the girls singing in the boat very early and then started the soca music when they got to the dock. In other words they were trying all different ways of having only one piece of music going at a time.

The sound of the girls singing wasn't enough to carry the scene. It's nice as a synch piece of music when you see it, but it was the wrong feeling: it didn't have that surge of energy that they needed when we see this family arriving in the wilderness, about to start off on a great adventure. So finally after trying all these different ways, they said, what the hell: open up the pots and let it go; play them both at the same time!

Why was the picture editor Thom Noble involved in editing the music?

If the scene is a synch scene—such as when we hear on the sound track what the girls are singing on screen—the picture editor cuts the music. And the picture editor always cuts at least one sound track, maybe two sound tracks, so that you know where there's going to be music. And if it's music that involves integrating on-camera singing with scored music then the picture editor has to do it because he decides when to cut to the music.

So the idea that there would be scored music throughout the entire scene and that there would be source music happening that you saw on-camera came from Peter and Thom. The actual realization of it—where the source music started and where the scored music started and what the relation between the two of them was, how long each one of them lasted, and how you got out of them—was finally realized in the mix.

Could you compare working methods at Fantasy with those in Hollywood?

What makes it different up here is that roles are not rigidly defined; the compartmentalization is not nearly as strong up here as it is in LA, which makes for a better film and a better sound track.

Why?

Because everybody's aware of everything else. Everybody knows how everything fits in, in relation to everything else: you're not only thinking of the dialogue. You're thinking of the dialogue in relation to the music. You're not only thinking of the Foley. And everybody, having mixed and cut everything else, has a sense of the picture as a whole, so you're not likely to be defending your personal territory; you're seeing how things fit into the picture as a whole. If the Foley doesn't work, well then you drop it. If the music isn't working, well then you drop it. If the Foley does work and you like it then you push it up a little bit. It's a lack of territoriality that I think is very good.

With all the sound broken up into dialogue, music and effects, there has to be a lot of communication between the various departments so that the dialogue department knows how the effects are going to cover up the hole where there's no dialogue, and so that when they meet it's going to be the right mesh. That's just the administrative stuff, but it's important. [Near the beginning of the picture] the sound of the jungle [for example] had to start out a certain intensity, then gradually change depending on what the story required. On **The Mosquito Coast** this overall coordination was done by Alan Splet, the supervising sound editor.

How do you compare the aesthetics of sound editing versus picture editing?

Most people understand how the picture can be edited—how you have many, many different scenes and how you put together one scene—because they see the cuts. People don't generally understand that the sound is also edited in as highly and maybe more sophisticated, a fashion as the picture. Basically, with the picture, you can put one cut up against another cut, or you can dissolve from one to the other, or you can have a visual effect and have two things happening at the same time. But ninety percent of what you see in a film is one cut up against another cut; once the cut has been made, very little happens until the next cut—in terms of editing.

So you could say that the picture is very one-dimensional: it starts, it goes along, there's a cut, and then it goes along again and there's another cut. The one thing happening is the cut. Sound, however, you could think

117

of it as being three-dimensional because you have one layer of sound, one actor talking, for instance, and then on top of that another actor is talking, and on top of that a clock ticking in the background, and then on top of that there could be another layer of sound, which could be the traffic outside, and then on top of that there will be another layer of sound, which could be a record player in the background, and then on top of that there will be another layer of sound, which could be somebody arguing in the room next door.

That's far more than three dimensions.

It's three-dimensional in the sense that it goes linearly and also it goes deep; in other words, there are many layers stacked up. So the sound is conceived of in layers, and each layer requires a lot of work and a lot of editing, in terms of taking the best take and matching it to the actors' lip movements so that it's always in synch. You might take the beginning lines of a take from take one and the ending lines from take four. Take one might have been recorded from a wide shot and have a lot of room ambience around it and take four might be a close-up and sound very intimate, but yet they have to be made to sound as though it were the same thing. It can get pretty complicated very quickly. So the dialogue editors have been preparing all of these layers of dialogue and then that comes into the mix.

How do you know when looping [when actors re-record dialogue in the studio] is necessary?

Peter, the director and the editor and the supervising dialogue editor (Vivien Hillgrove Gilliam) will have gone through the film—and sometimes I'll have said things, too, on the basis of the temp mixes—and Peter will say, "I don't like this performance. Let's loop this." Or "I don't want him to say 'Mother, I'm sorry.' I want him to say 'I didn't mean it.'" So we'll have to bring the actor in to loop that line.

What if it's a tight shot and the lips are visible. Can you still loop lines?

It depends. You can cheat a little bit. For example, during the storm sequence in **The Mosquito Coast** Harrison is in the water yelling at the top of his lungs through this hurricane. The synch line is, "Don't worry, Mother it's a boat. Lash the twins to the deck." Peter wanted him to say, "Don't worry, Mother, it'll float. Lash the twins to the deck." So if you look very closely you can see he's not saying "boat," he's saying "float." So you loop the whole line "Don't worry, Mother, it will float. Lash the twins to the deck." But the reading and the intensity is always better in the original, so what you do is you just take the word "float." You cut out the word "boat" from the production, when he said it, and you put in the word "float" from the studio and then you have to match them, so that one word, recorded here at high-and-dry, warm Fantasy, sounds like it was recorded on location in the middle of a hurricane.

How do you see sound functioning in a movie?

The job that sound does in a motion picture is manifold. One of the things it does is tell the story through the dialogue. That's a very obvious straightforward thing that sound does. It also creates the space in which the picture exists by creating an ambience, a bed or a space, if you will, that the dialogue and the other important sounds sit in and live in. It's like the room that the action is happening in. Sound also lends emotional emphasis to the story

119

that's happening. This is done most conventionally through the use of music: when there is a particularly scary moment, it will be underscored with scary music. In addition the sound effects can lend emotional support to the movie. In **The Right Stuff**, for example, there is this loud overpowering roar when the rockets take off; the men who are sitting on top of these giant bombs seem even more heroic because you **feel** the power of the rockets that they're trying to control. In something like **The Mosquito Coast** when Allie first gets to the jungle, the sounds of nature are overwhelming: you hear a completely untamed jungle with parrots and monkeys and bugs and birds. So you get a sense of this one man struggling against nature, and there are several scenes where nature overwhelms him. When they first arrive there's a scene where Allie and Mother are laughing after their first day of work and as you pull farther and farther back the laugh gets smaller and smaller and the sounds of nature completely overpower their laughter; it's a way of indicating that even though it may seem that they are making a heroic effort, they're really up against a huge jungle that they just can't begin to dominate.

How much of the mixing process is a purely technical one for you?

I tend to divide mixing into two aspects. One is the psychology of mixing and the interaction of the people and the other is the technical aspect of doing it. At this point I spend eighty percent on the psychology and talking to people and twenty percent on doing it. You can do anything you want. It's like playing an instrument—you just play the notes! But the important thing is how you play the notes, what the feeling is behind it, how you got there, and how you relate to the orchestra as a whole. Unless you're playing solo.

Do you ever play solo?

Oh, yes. If there's a long section with no effects, no music, just dialogue, that's the equivalent of playing solo. By that time it's already been prepared in the dialogue pre-mix, so all I have to do is sit there and let it play and make fine adjustments.

It's very boring to work alone. I don't like to work alone at all, I always want to have somebody else there. More often than not it will be the dialogue editor for the reel I'm working on: it will just be the two of us. We bounce back and forth: "How did that sound?" "Did that sound good?" "Did you like that?" "Why don't we do this?" "Well, I don't know." "Well, I think it's a good idea, let's try it." "OK, let's put this in as an alternate."

A large part of my job is as a translator. Some directors will say, "This isn't working for me," when you're dealing with a scene with dialogue, effects, and music. "Something's not right." It's my job to draw him out to find out specifically what isn't working for him. What aspect is not working? My job is to translate that into sound terms—for example, the music isn't working, or the effects aren't working. And then to figure out what it is about the music or the dialogue or the effects that isn't working—what can we change and how can we make it better? The end result of all of that will be that I will suggest, "Let's move this pot [the volume control] up from here to here and then bring it down again." If I'm in synch with the director I can say after a take, "Well, I think that maybe Harrison's line should be brought up just a little bit." And he'll say, "Yeah, yeah, that's right, that's just what I was thinking."

Reading his mind.

Yeah, reading his mind, or not just reading his mind

121

but responding the same or being in the same place where there's a lot of unspoken understanding about what's important, about whether or not something is working, so that the ideas that you have resonate with each other—which is where Peter and I got to after a while in the final mix. I would say something, and he would say, "Yeah, I was just thinking about that." Or he would say something, and it had been in the back of my mind as something to bring up.

It often happens among people who have been in the film business for a certain number of years [that they] have developed a sensitivity that is similar; it's a matter of developing similar sensitivities and similar aesthetic ideals. It doesn't mean that the film is going to be any better, because you can have exactly the opposite extreme and still come out with a good film. You can have somebody who is ready to spit all over you, and still come out with a good sound track, or you can have somebody who is totally in synch, who loves working with the people who he's with, and still have a good track. What's different is the work experience, the process, not the result. In order to continue working at this you have to get your rewards from the process, from the day to day work of it. You can't get your rewards from once every other year or so, going down to the Academy Awards for one day. You can't get your rewards from seeing the film in the theater when it's done. There's nothing in those one or two days that will justify spending months in a dark room looking at the same thing over and over again. So it's the process of making the film and the interaction with the people you're working with that make it worthwhile.

Which part of your work do you enjoy the least?

The part I enjoy the least, the part that is the most frustrating, is having to fix really bad sound that doesn't have to be so bad. One of the things that's really ironic is that we've got more and more advanced digital technology that's used to salvage poorer and poorer original recordings. The part that I enjoy the least on the technical side of it is having to salvage bad recordings. In **The Mosquito Coast,** for instance, we had to work very hard on Harrison's death scene on the boat. The original synch production sound, which was recorded on location, went with the takes they used. The sound was bad: it had a lot of water lapping and flopping. It was very distracting and very difficult to maintain the intimate, close mood of this guy lying down, giving his death speech to Mother and to Charlie. He doesn't think he's dying, but everybody thinks he is.

It never really worked for Peter. So he felt in order to make the scene stronger he had to have music, and that in order to have music in reel eleven to lead up to it he had to have music in reel 10 during the storm sequence. So they brought Harrison in to do ADR [Automatic Dialogue Replacement aka looping], and they ADR'd the whole scene, which was very difficult because [in the scene] he was lying down—he had just been shot—he was speaking quietly, and his throat was constricted. We tried all kinds of different ways of reproducing that: Harrison tried lying down and putting the mike up close, but he couldn't see the screen. He went through many gyrations trying to capture the intensity and the emotion he'd had during the production situation on the boat.

How long did you work on it?

Two or three days in the studio just for that scene.

What finally worked?

When we played the ADR version for Peter it was OK,

123

but it just didn't have the resolution and the impact of what he had wanted. He thought that the ending was nice, but it still wasn't solid. So then Vivien [Gilliam] and Laurel [Ladevich], the ADR editor, decided that this wasn't going to work and that they would have to go back through all the production takes and see if they could find words and phrases that didn't have the water lapping on them. So they went back through all the old production takes and managed to piece together a performance a word and a phrase at a time, scraping in and out around the water laps. They were able to maintain the intensity of the emotional expression that Peter was after, but had stripped away all the water blocks which were so distracting.

There were four or five alternates, so we sat down and picked the best readings four or five feet at a time, scene by scene. It was always a compromise between cleanest sound and best performance. And then we had to add in some of the ADR lines for which there were no alternates that were clean. Then you go through and you mix it all together.

How was Peter participating in this process?

He had seen all the synch stuff. He knew what the bad things were, he knew what the ADR was, he hadn't yet heard this new version. Then we played it for him. He was completely blown away: the entire end of the movie changed, because we had managed to preserve so much of the original intensity of Harrison's performance. Having achieved this clean, intense, non-distracting version of the end death scene meant to Peter that now the movie finally came together, that it was working, that you could finally get into Harrison and concentrate on the subtleties of his performance. He had thought that we would have to do it in ADR and if you do it in ADR you

124

lose ninety percent of what the original performance was about.

So having achieved this then we said, "Well, we can lose the music in reel eleven now, when they're drifting down the stream, because it's so quiet and his performance is so powerful that we don't need it. And taking out the music in reel eleven we don't have to have the music in the storm because it's not adding anything." So this one change at the end had its repercussions and echoed back all the way through the film.

8
Cotton Club
Sound design
for a Coppola period musical

Richard Beggs
(part one)

Richard Beggs' career in sound is a classic story of being in the right place at the right time. During the 1960s, San Francisco was a mecca for nascent rock 'n' roll musicians thirsty for stardom. Beggs saw an opportunity to develop an early fascination with sound into a potential business. And so, at virtually the amateur level, he began recording demo reels for budding young rock bands. This was a subsistence level occupation, but as Beggs' skills (and those of the bands he worked for) improved, his income increased. In the late '70s Beggs' studio occupied space in Francis Coppola's post production building. Picture editing and sound mixing on **Apocalypse Now** were commencing, and Beggs was hired to work as part of this team.

Since the early 1980s, Richard Beggs has been sound designer on all of Francis Coppola's feature films, usually doubling as re-recording mixer [until **Tucker** (1988)]. He also holds the distinction of having worked with Coppola longer than any member of the Zoetrope filmmaking team. In addition, he has been re recording mixer on 21 other generally more conventional theatrical features with other directors.

As part of the Coppola/Zoetrope post production team,

Beggs helped implement a number of Coppola innovations for the time in the use of feature film sound production. These include: use of two-inch 24-track audio technology in the sound mixing process and an automated sound mixing board; discussed below, they remain important signposts on the way to today's digital audio workstation technology. (Both innovations were introduced in 1977 on **Apocalypse Now**).

The Coppola/Zoetrope team has long been known in the film industry for being innovative and for its willingness to take risks, but general recognition of its contributions of making the job of the filmmaker an easier, less costly one, has been slow to come. Indeed, an editorial piece in the industry bible, **Variety**, once compared Coppola to Lee De Forest (inventor of television) who never received recognition for his contributions to communications technology nor society at large.

Precis

Job of the sound designer, how Beggs works with Coppola, mixer's responsibilities, versus Hollywood union post production sound crews, greatest challenge of **Cotton Club** *involved trade-off between artistic intent, technical requirements and good craftsmanship, dialogue/background music problem, conceptual framework for editing musical numbers, versus plotline, description of post production organization of* **CC**, *difficulty of getting source musical numbers synchronized to action on screen, comparison to* **Rumblefish** *and* **One from the Heart** *post production.*

Richard Beggs credits

Apocalypse Now ** (1979) Francis Coppola
No Nukes (1979) Julian Schlossberg,
    Danny Goldberg
Zulu Dawn (1979) Douglas Hickox
The Island (1980) Michael Ritchie
One from the Heart (1981) Francis Coppola
The Outsiders (1983) Francis Coppola
D.C. Cab (1983) Joel Schumacher
Mike's Murder (1983) James Bridges
Rumblefish (1983) Francis Coppola
Repo Man (1984) Alex Cox
Ghostbusters (1984) Ivan Reitman
Cotton Club (1984) Francis Coppola
Critters (1986) Stephen Herek
Modern Girls (1986) Jerry Kramer
Nutcracker—the Motion Picture (1986)
    Carroll Ballard
Gardens of Stone (1987) Francis Coppola
Spaceballs (1987) Mel Brooks
Walker (1987) Alex Cox
Dirty Rotten Scoundrels (1988) Frank Oz
Rainman (1988) Barry Levinson
Tucker: The Man and His Dream (1988)
    Francis Coppola
Avalon (1990) Barry Levinson
Cry-Baby (1990) John Waters
The Godfather Part III (1990) Francis Coppola
Bugsy (1991) Barry Levinson
Single White Female (1992) Barbet Schroeder
Toys (1992) Barry Levinson
Rising Sun (1993) Phil Kaufman
Sleepers (1996) Barry Levinson

Why didn't the credit sound designer exist before (longtime Coppola associate) Walter Murch virtually single handedly invented it?

Movie making has always been compartmentalized. Movie making is divided into all these little fiefdoms or kingdoms: there's the camera department, there's costume, there's the art department, there's the production recordist, there's the post production mixer. And all of these people have their own area of expertise and their own order of importances and their own idea of how they relate to the picture. It's amazing that all the people get together and agree to get anything done. Even in the worst movies—the worst movie is a miracle.

Sound and picture and music have been traditionally very separate little kingdoms, jealously guarded and somewhat autonomous, until they get to the mixing stage where, traditionally, the composer might show up, the picture editor shows up. All of these people don't necessarily have the same idea about what's going to happen.

Traditionally, music and sound effects have been a kind of loyal opposition. The composer frequently takes the position that, "My music is being buried in sound effects." The sound effects editor says: "In this scene the music is taking all of the action. What is the point of my cutting all of this stuff if nobody's going to hear it?" And the mixer is sitting there listening to these two people trying to mediate. The director, if he has the presence of mind, will say what he wants. Everybody has to go along with that.

Well, the sound design idea is that there is a person who, in addition to balancing the three aspects of the sound track—dialogue, music and effects—has an overall view and understanding of the picture and the director's intentions. And that person is a creative collaborator in the filmmaking process. The sound designer works to integrate these various elements of the sound track before they get to the dubbing stage.

What frequently happens is that the composer never talks to the sound effects people, the effects people never ask the composer what he has in mind. There are eight or nine people on a movie cutting a gigantic sound effects scene. The composer has scored a gigantic piece of music for 110 musicians. When you get on the sound mixing stage you discover you can't use both of them. What do you do? Theoretically, the sound designer is there to avoid or at least mitigate this situation by seeing ahead and working around it.

He knows by talking to the composer and the director that, for example, in this scene it makes more sense for the music to carry it. So, then he goes and talks to the sound effects editor and says: "In this scene we're going to play it like this. So, don't cut the sound so heavy, etc." He develops or controls the concept of the track and integrates it with the picture.

Can you give me some examples of creative interaction between you and Coppola on *Cotton Club*?

He basically leaves me alone. I pretty much work by myself. We talk initially about some directions or concepts or feeling and then I come up with a group of ideas and rough them in. We'll have a screening, he'll make a few notes and say: "Yes, no, maybe." I will work on that information. Sometimes, we will disagree but we invariably resolve the problem by mutual agreement.

Has that been the way it's been on all of your collaborations?

Basically, all of my pictures with him have been that way to one degree or another.

Other directors aren't accustomed to or don't want to relinquish that much control or don't have that much interest beyond making sure that certain fundamental things sound right—whether the music and dialogue are at the right level and relation to each other and the effects don't hide the dialogue. Those are the basic considerations most directors have.

Francis has a real interest in sound as a partner in the image and wants it to work on different levels and do things.

How does that difference in attitude on the part of Coppola influence the way you work—for example, are you less creative on a picture like *Repo Man*?

Well, yes. On those pictures I function more as a craftsman and exercise taste but without the autonomy I'm given on Francis' pictures. On **D.C. Cab** there was a music cue that didn't work and I said: "Why don't we use part of that cue in the other reel, instead of using it here?" The director said: "OK." But this was definitely an exception. Basically, you mix what's put in front of you. I don't control or choose the effects. I may make suggestions but that is the extent of involvement. I don't say: "This is unacceptable, do it again." Basically, a mixer in Hollywood is like a service: you go to a dubbing stage, you bring all your material and these guys just do what you tell them to do.

You wouldn't send a sound effects editor down to re-record material?

Well, you might ask him: "Could we get something better?" It would be a technical decision. Artistic decisions are usually the prerogative of the director or the editor in those situations.

But with Coppola, is it your capacity?

Yes. With Francis I'm basically the sound director, sound designer. I'm more or less responsible for the sound track and everything you hear in it, subject to Francis' approval.

Don't you exercise a good deal of technical quality control on any picture?

On any picture a mixer does that. A mixer can say: "This is distorted, I'd like another door slam." But then you get in to the area of whether or not you even want a door slam. Or maybe instead of having a literal door you might want the door of a vault closing for artistic reasons because it might sound more interesting to you. Those are creative decisions and those aren't normally the mixers purview. But under Francis I can make those decisions and experiment with the track.

Usually on a picture you have the supervising sound effects editor, he more or less picks and supervises the effects. The editors cut them at his behest, the mixer mixes them, and the director oversees the whole proposition.

My concept of the sound designer—how I prefer to work—is that I work closely with or function as a supervising sound editor and as a mixer. I prepare and cut some of my own effects. I build my own materials for special sequences that I want to be directly responsible for creating. I work closely with the composer so our work is integrated. I make no distinction between effects and music. So what happens—and why Hollywood is so weird—is I will cross three or four union categories.

What was your greatest challenge while working on *Cotton Club*?

The fundamental mixer problem on **Cotton Club** was the music/dialogue issue, how to play the club sequences successfully. We were faced with a difficult problem because the actors didn't loop their lines as if they were in a noisy environment.

Is that because of a mistake in shooting?

No. It's because of extremely complicated production techniques. It's a trade-off between artistic intent, technical requirements and limitations, and good craftsmanship.

When the lines were originally performed the background sounds (band, crowds, etc.) were relatively low, not at all what you would expect in a loud night club so the actors tended not to project. The loops were performed similarly. Francis was also striving for a certain quality of performance. Performance is the primary goal. Technical or craft issues fall into place to support the performance.

So, how can you have crowds and blaring music at peak level and still have this dialogue remain intelligible? It's very difficult. So, the actors act in an environment that will be quite different on the screen. You would have to say to them: "OK, you have to speak loudly because you're in a loud club." It's hard to get them to do it and be natural so it's let go to be solved later in post.

It's hard to explain. But when it's costing $75,000 a day in just extras it's hard to ask somebody: "Could you do a take where it looks like you're talking a little louder." Nobody wants to hear about it. Ninety-nine percent of this movie is looped. Almost everything you hear with the exception of three or four scenes is looped.

Well, doesn't that solve the problem where you were talking about the background sound in the nightclub scenes?

No, it doesn't because actors duplicate their original performance unless Francis wants the performance to change. This was the big problem in **Rumblefish**. Michael Rourke spoke in virtual whisper, **sotto voce**, almost all the time even if you were at the other end of the block.

Cotton Club's problems were similar, if not so severe. Whispers and **sotto voce** are always a problem especially in loud environments. People speak in your ear or very close if they want to communicate this way. You can't do that in the theater. You have to lower the background or make the whisper very loud. Loudness doesn't help that much though. **Sotto voce** and whispers are all bottom and top. There's no middle, no middle range to grab and punch through. The whisper can be at peak modulation, but imbedded in a loud background it cannot be heard. Whereas a normal voice at moderate level can be easily distinguished. Loudness does not equal intelligibility.

The looping on **Cotton Club** was pretty good. We didn't have the problems nearly that we had on **Rumblefish**, but the **sotto voce** performance is still there and you can only distort the performance so far in terms of the audience's credibility. They have to hear the dialogue. So you can only make the dialogue so loud and still have it be natural. Then you say: "Now we have to pull the music back. But where do we lose the feeling of the scene that they're in? How important is that compared to the strain the audience experiences attempting to follow the dialogue?"

Looping takes care of a lot of problems in terms of being able to control acoustical relationships. If you used production sound only you wouldn't have any choice, you'd have to take what you've got. In a musical, that's next to impossible.

Cotton Club is a musical by the very fact that more than 50% of its screen time is dominated by musical action. Taking that as a given, do you know what was the conceptual framework which governed how Cotton Club was cut?

There was much more music in it at one time, many more numbers. And one of the big problems editorially with the picture was balancing the desire to have as much music in these **Cotton Club** numbers as possible against the need to have a story line or a plot line that would keep the audience involved.

My feeling is that the problem of blending the music and the drama was very successfully solved: integrating the musical aspect into the story without having that "Here-is-a-number" feeling. The scene that comes closest to being a number is the hoofers' club sequence with all the old guys. It's one of the favorite scenes and it's there because it's so lovable and it builds atmosphere. It's not necessary for the plot. It's not exposition. All of the other numbers are rationalized by the plot.

I would like to get as clear a concept as possible of what you did on Cotton Club. For example, did this picture come to you with all the musical sequences already inserted in it?

The picture was cut and locked to sound track in New York City. It was brought to Napa [Coppola's California post production facility] for music pre-mix and final mix. Dialogue pre-mix was done at Lucasfilm. We screened and recut picture four times as a result of exhibitor previews in Chicago, San Jose, Boston and Seattle.

On this picture I did less than on any other picture I've done, mainly because the picture was an East Coast picture. I wasn't even going to work on it. I was brought in very late. By comparison on **Rumblefish** I worked very closely with Francis and the composer (Stewart Copeland) throughout the whole picture. In this case, the source music is a given—the stuff that's on screen, you're not going to move it, you can't change it, you can't take it out or move it unless the picture's lifted [read deleted] or moved.

The underscore worked by and large. It was done once and then was reorchestrated at Francis' request. I got in at that stage.

Once again by comparison, I worked a lot with the music editor on **Cotton Club** (Norman Hollyn). Obviously on a picture like this he's very important. There was an incredible amount of preparation and sheer physical effort spent to make sure that when it's all together the musicians we are seeing are playing in synch with the music we are hearing on the track. It sounds pretty basic but it's extremely difficult.

What was the time frame of the whole filmmaking process of *Cotton Club*?

Pre-production began in July of 1983. Francis began working on the script when I was finishing **Rumblefish**. They began shooting in September [1983]. They broke for Christmas with some pick-up shooting in January. February, March, April, May were all editorial [picture cutting]. Sound editorial and all of that stuff began in June and July. I started working on this picture in July.

My work with the sound editors consisted of a trip to New York where I discussed what we were after in building the sound track. I listened to some pre-mixes back there to make sure they were coming along all right. Usually, I prefer to hire all the sound editors myself and put together my own team. This being a New York production I had nothing to do with hiring them.

Francis is known as someone who has been endeavoring to bring new technologies into the use of film-making. To what extent do you think that his innovations or drive to innovate filmmaking have influenced the way you work?

Francis has given me carte blanche. His ideas are aesthetic and theoretical; they're not technical. When we first started working together in '79 he liked the way recording studios worked on 24-tracks and said: "Richard, can you work this way on a movie?" And I said: " Yeah, I don't know why not." And so we did it.

Coppola used a video system on *Cotton Club* to make pre-cuts of scenes at the end of shooting days. Did you see any of the video pre-cuts on *Cotton Club*, and did you use them in your work?

Only in terms of looking at them and preparing myself for what was coming. This picture was very conventional and I really didn't do very much of that. For instance, on **Rumblefish** and **One from the Heart** I got a video cut of the picture at a very early stage and began building and manipulating sound on 24-track to those pictures well in advance of the final mix. And would then take those elements on 24-track into the final mix locked to picture and use them. I'd work essentially in a recording studio building all this stuff. On **Cotton Club** there wasn't the necessity or the need to do it. The picture just wasn't structured that way. The track didn't have those requirements. It could have been done that way but it wasn't set up that way.

What has been the greatest single technological advance which has helped you work in film sound since you started in '79?

Automated mixing. I don't know any films other than Francis' films that I have worked on that have been mixed with automation. [Beggs is of course speaking of pictures made before 1984].

What are benefits of this system?

Repeatability. On a conventional mixing deck you have three mixers: dialogue, effects, and music. Nowadays you record on three separate recorders so that if the dialogue guy gets his stuff right he can sort of stop and then the music guy can work until he's ready and so on. And you can see the advantage of that.

Well, a lot of times you can be mixing a sequence and you have 25 or 30 elements coming in and you can get it almost right. But there's something that isn't quite right, you've rehearsed it four or five times. You've got it just about how you want it. Do you try to do it again and possibly lose what you've got and get the thing that is outstanding? Or do you just say: "It's as good as we can get it for now, it's not worth trying to do it again because it will never be as good," and go on?

With automation you save everything you want and you can go in at any one point and change any one aspect—when a reel goes down and then comes back up, and you have to punch in, which frequently happens, a line has to change. Especially in a master where all the effects and everything are going. You have to match on a big board conceivably as many as 90 elements, that when you punch in, the join is imperceptible. And so every level has to be what it was maybe three weeks or a month ago.

139

The automation will remember all these things for you in terms of level. Equalization is something else. We don't have automated equalization. But theoretically that should be in your head and it shouldn't be that far off.

Another big advantage is that you can do a lot of one-man mixing, which I like to do. Everything is stored in data. You don't really record anything. It's all in memory. Then I can work a little bit on music. And just jump back and forth constantly working and shaping the thing. Then you go back, push the button, and record it.

The automated board doesn't really save that much more time. It theoretically can, but I find I use the time it saves to do more and do it better. There's a reluctance on the part of people in the business to confront a piece of new equipment. The new is always threatening. And it shouldn't be.

8
Tucker: The Man and His Dream
Sound design for a dreamer

Richard Beggs
(part two)

With the making of **Tucker: The Man and His Dream** Francis Coppola realized a long-cherished dream to make a film about another dreamer—innovator and maverick Preston Tucker. In 1946 Tucker's dream was to design and market America's first completely new car in 50 years. Some of the car's innovations included aerodynamic styling, padded dash, pop-out windows, seat belts, fuel injection, and disc brakes—all radical ideas at the time. In the end financial and legal difficulties—some self-imposed, others the result of the Detroit auto establishment's conspiracy against him—prevented him from producing more than 50 cars. Ironically most remain road-worthy to this day. **Tucker** is the story of how that dream came to be realized.

Coppola choose his long-time sound designer, Academy Award winner Richard Beggs, to head the post production sound crew of the $30-million picture. And he hired British pop composer Joe Jackson to create a lively, brassy "scoring" music track, which owes much to the period depicted in the film.

Beggs and his sound crew divided their six month post production schedule between his San Francisco basement studio (for multi-track) and George Lucas' plush, exceedingly comfortable Skywalker Ranch. **Tucker** holds the distinction of having been the first feature film to be

141

mixed at the then newly opened facility. In general Beggs was pleased at the shakedown at Skywalker, and was especially glad to find technicians at his beck and call anytime tweaking was called for.

Precis

*Sound design of **Tucker** reflected idealized pre-WWII genre of American filmmaking, Beggs' method of developing sound design—acoustical signatures, air compressor example, effectiveness of this signature, functionality of sound between the conscious and the unconscious, compared to **Gardens of Stone** acoustical signatures, use of cartoon effect in **Tucker** garage sequence as character motif, origins of these effects.*

How did you create the sound design for *Tucker*?

The stylistic antecedents for the picture were discussed [during production]. The camera angles, the idealized family life, these elements all point in a certain direction. This was a genre of period films, that was looked at and talked about: the '30s and '40s American genre picture that dealt with American ideals and values à la **Mr. Smith Goes to Washington.**

The car thing/element is really, if you'll excuse the pun, a vehicle to carry these other considerations. How does this relate to sound? Rather than jump to conclusions or develop ideas completely early on, my tendency is to hold them back—not let them develop conceptually—and just keep the germ of the idea around. As I look at cuts of the picture, talk with Francis, or go on location, a lot of ideas occur to me, some small, some large. By that time I've seen the picture enough that certain thematic ideas may have presented themselves: acoustical signatures, something that might typify a certain scene or location, elements that will tie the picture together much like music would. And I think about how those sounds can be used for dramatic effect in those sequences rather than for just what they are.

For instance in the shop adjacent to Tucker's home in Ypsalanti [Michigan], which is a fairly well equipped automotive shop with a lot of hydraulic equipment—jacks and hoists. A common sound you hear in those places, though we never see one in the movie, is an air compressor. It makes a rhythmic pumping sound: it starts up, goes for a while, and then when the tank reaches capacity it shuts down with a very characteristic sound. Then it's quiet for a while, either until the pressure drops naturally or it's used with some tool and it turns on with a characteristic sound, revs up, runs at speed, et cetera.

So I seized on that as a possibility. In this movie I was hard pressed to find elements that I could use like that—rhythmic, acoustic elements that tied to manufacturing and cars that could be used dramatically. I used it in that sense in several scenes to create a kind of tension. Like in the scene where Tucker explodes after Alex Tremulus [the car's designer] is almost crushed by the car. This device [or effect] is used at the beginning of the scene then stops at a very critical point. The fact that it stops helps to create a kind of ambience and mood that is dramatic in nature.

Specifically what function did you see the effects playing in this sequence?

We come from a very relaxed, martini sequence with (Joe Jackson's) adult martini music. Abe, [Preston

Tucker's partner], who is visiting Tucker and his family, brings his daughter a dress. They have a little toast, everything seems to be going fine. Then Tucker's son comes in and there's this emergency. We cut to the garage. It's like a pressure cooker—there's lots of hammering and banging. They're way behind deadline; there's all this mechanical cacophony. One of the effects is that of the air compressor: **de-de-de-de-de-de-de**. As the scene progresses, the tension mounts between the characters. And then the car falls. Alex is almost killed. Almost all the sound in the garage stops because all the workers have gathered around. But the air compressor keeps going, it isn't something that somebody turns off. The music is stopped.

So the only thing that's going is the **de-de-de-de-de-de-de**, this insistent air compressor with the dialogue. As the dialogue continues there are altercations and animosity between characters and the sound actually builds in intensity and finally Tucker explodes in this semi-psychotic episode—emotionally he's pretty out there. He explodes and hits this bulletin board with his fist. When he does that, I took processed sounds of metal being hit and some gongs and underscored his fists hitting the board, which gave a more dramatic impact. And then as soon as that begins dying away the compressor goes into its off cycle: **do-do-do-do-do-do**...and the room collapses into absolute dead silence and all you hear are his feet scraping and then the dialogue resumes with just one person.

At that point Vittorio [Storaro, Director of Photography], interestingly enough, changes the color in the room as if a cloud had come over the sun outside and changed what was a warmer golden hue into a depressed gray. That was an observation that I made later—that these things were all working together.

Why do you think that particular effect works?

In no particular order of importance: the sound is rationalized because of the context of the scene—that is something you would have in that place; it's organic to the scene. Then the sound has a relentless percussive nature: it functions as music—this constant odd staccato pattern creates a kind of nervous tension. When it stops and the way it stops, it's an obvious relaxing effect—it has an exhaling sound. It's like **ahhhhhhhhhhhh**. It has a kind of anthropomorphic aspect to it. It's very subtle. A lot of people probably won't even notice it. If you take it out, the scene isn't nearly as effective.

That's the way sound should work. It functions not in the unconscious but somewhere between the unconscious and the conscious.

By contrast the way we created the track for **Gardens Of Stone** [a Vietnam-era story set at the military base where soldiers' corpses are processed for internment] was much more obvious because there were a lot of sound signatures or motifs there—it was such an eccentric and unusual acoustical environment. **Tucker** wasn't nearly so special. It just had these cars and people working on them so there wasn't any acoustical pattern that would hold it all together.

What was eccentric about *Gardens*?

Here was a place where you hear horses, hooves, and wagon wheels in a modern setting all the time. You hear a lot of marching and heel clicking, the constant bark and shout of commands, drums and bands outside rehearsing. So right away you had this fabric, this tapestry, which you can dip into and use and grab little pieces and threads to weave through the whole plot because that's the environment of the military base.

But in **Tucker**, they live in the country, they have a

house, there are some birds. The garage next to the house, where they're making the car, is where there's any kind of consistent thematic sound pattern. These guys are working with tools, hammers, hoists. So the sound of making the car—whenever we're out in that room I tended to stylize and push that. There are a lot of off-camera effects that create that drive forward. For example, the first time we go into the garage Joe [Jackson] has this piece of music playing that's a montage sequence and I used valve grinders, a hydraulic punch press, the compressor.

This sequence is toward the beginning of the picture, when the assembly crew really gets going and they start building the car, the first shot in the garage. It cuts away to Abe selling the car and ends with Jimmy driving the test chassis around the back yard. All those sounds were used against the music to supply the textures—industry-on-parade-in-your-backyard. At one point Eddie [one of Tucker's mechanics] strikes a hammer in response to something Tucker has told him. And I inserted a comic element, there's a **boooing boooing** with a ridiculous slide whistle sequence. It's a cartoon effect. It's not unlike during the premiere sequence [when the Tucker car is first shown to the public] where I used a comic squirt for the oil coming out of the car before it catches on fire. There's a **boink, boink, boink**. It's a ridiculous sound, nothing really sounds like that. We got it from a cartoon library.

I used a lot of those effects in **One from the Heart**. A lot of the stylistic preoccupations of **Tucker** go back to **One from the Heart**. For me **Tucker** is a more refined version of what I did on **One from the Heart**. The music wasn't as important [on **One from the Heart**], but in general the texture and the way the sound was treated was similar.

One from the Heart used a lot of exaggerated, on-the-edge-of-comedy, if not broad comedy, effects. A guy would sit down on an old couch and the spring would go

boinnnnnnnng. Preston Sturges did that in his comedy films in the '40s.

Eddie [in **Tucker**] is a comic character, if there's any in the movie, and to use these comic sounds in conjunction with him underscores his character and his point of view. He's the comic relief in the picture. So, in conjunction with him I've taken the liberty of using these broader goofball sounds, which are unnatural sounds.

Did you play off that comic relief from what you found in the script?

I couldn't get any of that from reading the script. These things occurred to me while I was watching the picture. When I saw the first cuts I understood the style of the picture, what its antecedents were, and I realized that was a direction I could go in.

There's a slightly offbeat, quirky, American, if you will, aspect to this picture. There's a slight eccentricity to it. There's an innocence and naivete about this picture. And I approached the track from that point of view.

Did you and Francis discuss these comic elements in any detail?

No. The one clue he gave me and I think the only clue to what direction the track would take occurred when he said: "It can be zany."

9
Mishima
Sound design

Leslie Shatz

How does an American sound designer, who has never been to Japan and does not understand Japanese, go about creating the sound track for a Japanese-language feature film about the life and death of that country's foremost postwar cultural hero? Should he travel to Japan to learn something about Japanese culture before embarking on this project, or study the language and customs of this ancient, yet so modern people? And lastly, what would be the best hardware to utilize in creating raw sound for this potentially exotic track? These were some of the questions Leslie Shatz had to answer after co-producer, Tom Luddy, hired him to design the sound track for the controversial Japanese-American co-production, **Mishima**.

Initially, director Paul Schrader, provided Shatz with a complete script of this biographical study of Yukio Mishima—Japan's most acclaimed modern novelist, playwright, and author, who committed ritual suicide in 1970, while attempting a military coup at the Department of Defense.

Shatz's work began at the same time as the picture editor's, a rarity for Hollywood films, but fairly common for pictures post produced in the San Francisco area. (Post production for **Mishima** was done at Lucasfilm and Russian Hill Recording). One of the advantages of such an early entry onto the project was that Shatz was able to screen the partially edited workprint of **Mishima** almost as soon as it was assembled.

In the sections of the film based on Mishima's novels, Shatz discovered extraordinary visuals in the sets of

149

famed Japanese production designer Eiko Ishioka. "Her style is a super realistic one that is surreal. She uses extremely vivid colors and schematic props and archetypes to represent reality and represent ideas and images. It was her work that inspired mine; this was my main preparation for my sound design," said Shatz. (He decided he had all the material he needed for his sound design at hand, and did not need to travel to Japan, after all).

To this ten-year veteran of post production film sound work, the task ahead was clear: to create a textured, complex sound design analogous to Ishioka's sets.

What hardware would help him create these "archetypes of sound"? On the advice of musician and synthesist friends, Shatz decided to explore creating sounds on equipment he had never used before, the Yamaha DX-7 Synthesizer. The DX-7 had been recommended for its unusual capability to imitate natural sounds yet create sounds which were disjointed from reality, as Ishioka's sets were disjointed from the reality of Mishima's life in the film.

"So I got the DX-7, put it in my editing room and spent two agonizing weeks learning how to program this device. It was really agony. It was like going to school again. I started pushing buttons and for days and days and days got nothing. I got disappointed. I kept playing the cricket sound [which he had successfully experimented with] and thinking: 'We have this. There must be more possibilities.'"

In the following interview, sound designer Leslie Shatz discusses his solution to this creative block, as well as many aspects of the collaborative filmmaking process on **Mishima**.

Precis

Use of Eiko Ishioka's surreal sets as analog for sound design for **Mishima,** *use of Yamaha DX-7 synthesizer, resolving creative block, working with director Paul Schrader, scratch mix, working with Philip Glass' pre-recorded score early on in post production, importance of collaboration.*

Leslie Shatz's credits

Apocalypse Now (1979) Francis Coppola
Dragonslayer (1981) Matthew Robbins
One from the Heart (1982) Francis Coppola
Rumblefish (1983) Francis Coppola
The Black Stallion Returns (1983) Robert Dalva
Once Upon a Time in America (1984)
        Sergio Leone
Dune (1984) David Lynch
Mishima (1985) Paul Schrader
True Stories (1986) David Byrne
Tough Guys Don't Dance (1987) Norman Mailer
Catch Me If You Can (1989) Stephen Sommers
The Fly II (1989) Chris Walas
Heart of Midnight (1989) Matthew Chapman
War of the Roses (1989) Danny DeVito
Winter People (1989) Ted Kotcheff
Ghost (1990) Jerry Zucker
Henry and June (1990) Phil Kaufman
Don't Tell Mom the Babysitter's Dead (1991)
        Stephen Herek
Ernest Scared Stupid (1991) John Cherry
Prayer of the Roller Boys (1991) Rick King
Rambling Rose (1991) Martha Coolidge

Brain Donors (1992) Dennis Dugan
Bram Stoker's Dracula (1992) Francis Coppola
Crossing the Bridge (1992) Mike Binder
Wind (1992) Carroll Ballard
Dragon: The Bruce Lee Story (1993) Rob Cohen
Indian Summer (1993) Mike Binder
The Opposite Sex and How to Live with Them
(1993) Matthew Meshekoff
By the Sword (1993) Jeremy Kagan
The Secret Garden (1993) Agnieszka Holland
Angie (1994) Martha Coolidge
Even Cowgirls Get the Blues (1994)
      Gus Van Sant
Rudyard Kipling's Jungle Book (1994)
      Stephen Sommers

Give us an example of how you were influenced by Ishioka's sets to do a specific sound effect, sound design, or sound sequence on *Mishima*?

The entire concept for the sound for her sequences was derived by the application of the same concept that she used: I wanted to find archetypes of naturalistic sounds and to apply them very specifically and achieve a heighten sense of realism, because that would be the only proper companion to Ishioka's sets.

I managed to program the DX-7 to make a nightingale that not only was realistic sounding but one I could perform. I could play it in many different ways. Depending on how hard I pressed the key or which key I pressed, I would get a different nightingale. That's just one effect and at that point things started to open up for me.

Do you understand why?

I don't know, I guess it's part of the creative process. All of the days that I felt were spent wasted and just pushing buttons and farting around, I guess on some level I did begin to understand on a deeper level what this machine was doing.

I think if you talk to anybody about the DX-7, they'll tell you programming it is a nightmare. There are guys whose specialty is just to do that. At many points I had thought: "Oh, God! It's worth it for me to pay my own money to somebody to bail me out of this mess."

But finally I understood how it worked. I started to get wind and wind chimes and different kinds of birds and frogs and ducks and owls and seagulls. These were to be part of the sound design for the section of the film dealing with the first novel, which was **The Temple of the Golden Pavilion**. There was one line that always stood out in my mind: "The beauty of nature is sheer hell." It was a line that this one cynical acolyte said to a young boy as they were walking down this beautiful path.

And so I thought that line was a great banner to keep in my mind as I tried to program these sounds. I was making realistic sounds but when you got them all together it sounded like some kind of a prison that these people were in. The beauty was so sweet and treacly and sickening that I felt that it conveyed that concept.

How much of this was suggested by Schrader?

Not a single thing. In fact, I hid what I was doing from everybody because I thought they would laugh and would say: "Come on, get this stuff out of here. We've got to get down to real work." One day Schrader came in to the mixing room and was just standing there. He leaned against the synthesizer. He didn't know what it was. And the sound of a car revving up came out of the speaker.

153

Schrader started looking around and asked: "What's going on?"

And then he looked back and I put in the keyboard and he pressed the key and laughed. He realized this was what I'd been doing. And I said: "I got a bunch of other stuff here, too." He said: "Oh, wow! That's great, fantastic."

I really felt that after all this effort I wanted to sit down and play him every sound and say: "Gee, Paul, this one took me two weeks. This one took me a week. What do you think of this one?" But he wasn't that kind of guy. He wanted me to get the work done and that was it.

How long did this preparatory phase last?

A month and a half, maybe two months. All the while I was trying to lay the groundwork for the rest of the work and we had scratch mixes. Scratch mixes are becoming the bane of the sound designer's existence. First, they [producers and/or directors] want to show the movie in its bare form and then directors get an itch—and rightfully so. They want it to be as good as it possibly can when they project it for themselves and for other people. So, they say: "Do you have the sound of a door opening and closing, a car going by..." Soon, it becomes more expanded and you start cutting actual sequences of sound and you realize: "Hey, I don't want to do crummy work that's going to be seen by anybody." You can't just say in the screening in the middle of a terribly cut sequence: "Oh, well, this is just for the scratch mix."

So, you start having to lavish large amounts of labor to do it. Then the minute the film is projected the scratch mix is obsolete because they will go back to the cutting room and make changes.

And this was complicated because Philip Glass' music is fairly continuous so you can't cut the scratch mix. So, we would remix the scratch mix and cut all the elements. I was trying to juggle all of that while I was making these sounds with the synthesizer. I wasn't getting a lot of sleep because then I would be remixing the scratch mix at ten at night.

But the big advantage it did have for me was that rather than waiting till the very end to have Paul hear these sounds, I would slip one or two of them in these various scratch mixes, so that people would hear them and would become comfortable with them. At first people were very uncomfortable and would say: "Well, what's that? What is that sound? I don't like that."

I guess I was becoming sort of woebegone because I didn't know if I was on the right track or if what I was pursuing was valid. And finally we had a screening for George Lucas and Francis Coppola [co-executive producers of **Mishima**]. They had several comments about the film and one of them was that they thought these sounds were great and that they wanted more of them.

The sound was one of the elements that was going to differentiate the novel sections from the rest of the film or at least that's the way Tom Luddy [co-producer of **Mishima**] related it to me. It made my spirits very buoyant. After that screening Paul came up to me and said: "Do as much of it as you can." Whereas before he was sort of standing on the sidelines, now he was embracing it fully.

So that's some sort of a consensus?

Yes, at that point it was. When Francis and George agree on something it becomes a consensus very quickly.

Well, how does this compare to previous films you've worked on in terms of the way you went about creating sound and experimenting and researching?

Normally, I will sit with a director who will have very

155

specific comments and concepts at various points in the reel: "I want this there and that there." He'll probably want to hear very specific sounds and at that point you go to work in a pretty linear fashion. You gather the sounds you need. You get a crew of people together who can work fast or well. You record Foley and then you go to the mix.

But on this picture [**Mishima**] the director never sat down with me to spot it. He never communicated his vision of the sound track of the movie, which I think was evolving all the way along. He wasn't familiar with the mechanical aspects of the sound track so I was on my own. Also the budget on the film was low so I had to do things in cost cutting ways wherever I could. For instance, when my assistant became the Foley walker and then he became the dialogue editor. I trained him in these various tasks. We normally record Foley on 10 or 12 tracks and it's a big chore to cut it and mix it.

We did the Foley at a place called Russian Hill Recording [San Francisco]. They were very cooperative with us and it was quite an encouraging environment to work in. They recorded to two-inch multitrack tape so we weren't limited by the number of tracks that we used. We then did Foley in the normal spread out fashion of up to 12 tracks per reel. We ended up getting the most precise synch on the Foley stage that we could and then we mixed all the tracks down. We mixed 12 tracks down to two tracks; in some cases we have a third track, but not usually. Then the editor just had eight tracks to cut. It was really great because if the synch did become really screwy we could go back to the 24-track and transfer those little bits that were wrong. We didn't have to do that, though.

Were you were given Glass' prerecorded music track early on?

He was able to do a temp version of his score for the entire movie within the third week of editing, which is pretty amazing. This wasn't just him playing the piano; it was with bells and strings, all of the instruments that represented what was going to be there in the final performance. And considering that the score runs so continuously throughout the movie, this was such a boon I don't think the film could have been edited or created in the way that it was without this music on hand so early in that stage of the filmmaking.

I would hope that all composers would be able to move in that direction. So often in a film you work and edit the picture and cut the sound effects and, at the very last minute, they bring in a score that they've spent hundreds of thousands of dollars on but have only heard once or twice or three times. So there's a mad scramble to try to figure out how it fits with the movie.

We had a complete rendition of the score three weeks into the editing process. Then we cut the score and the picture one against the other. The picture would dictate cuts in the music and the music would dictate certain picture cuts. Then nearing the final cut of the film these notes and cassette of the way the music was applied to the picture were sent back to Mr. Glass. Then he conducted and recorded the real instruments to make the real score onto multitrack.

We brought that back on multitrack to Lucasfilm, where we mixed the music down to the picture, which is a technique that was used exclusively in the old days when music was recorded to three- and four-track and it wasn't a big deal. Now it's not done so much anymore.

Again, in this case, I don't see how we could have done it any other way. We used the cue lock and locked the film recorder at Lucasfilm and the projector in the big room up to the multitrack downstairs. It was kind of a nightmarish session because the cue lock had many problems. But still what we achieved was a tailored mix and a tailored cut of the music because in many cases the music had to be trimmed or expanded. It was done with the director, composer, the editor, the music producer and music conductor and myself there, so there were no surprises.

Nowadays music is usually delivered on the mixing stage as a three-track—left, center, and right—which gives the director no option on how to play it. I think that's a mistake because the mixdown of the music is usually just as critical as the mixdown of the sound effects or the dialogue. There's so much flexibility in the way you mix music in terms of the instruments you choose to feature or, perhaps, even leave out.

On the movie I'm working on now [**The Journey of Natty Gann** at Disney Studios] the director likes a particular music cue very well but there's one instrument in it—a marimba—that he hates. The composer gave him a completely mixed down track so his only option was to drop the cue, which was foolish, so he's going to go back and remix it.

On *Mishima*, how many tracks did you deliver to Schrader?

It varied because certain reels were more complex, but we probably had 50 tracks of sound for any particular reel. There are so many elements involved: dialogue, ADR, Foley. There's a whole set of real sound effects that had to support the real part of the film—the black and white and the biographical section. Then there were the stereo sound effects which were the ones that I was creating.

See, they had never planned mixing the movie in stereo. They had planned mixing it in mono because it was a low budget film and they had the notion that it would be too expensive to mix it in stereo. All the while I felt it was ridiculous to make this movie with a strong element from music and strong element from sound in mono. I was planning on a stereo mix regardless of what they said, which is why I prepared my sound effects in stereo.

What we ended up doing was having the parts that dealt with Mishima's final day and of Mishima's biography in mono. We spread the sound image to stereo whenever we entered the world of the novels, which was another way we distinguished the novel sections from the rest of the film.

Was that your idea?

Yes, it was, and Paul took to it very well.

From what I know about the Hollywood film industry it's hard to image that anyone would be given the kind of freedom to research and explore original concepts for sound design like you did on *Mishima*. Could you imagine working that way down there?

Every film is different.

Have you ever worked on a film that way in Hollywood?

This one [**Natty Gann**] was sort of like that but I snuck it in on them. I never told anybody: "Hey, I'm just going to go off and do sound design and all of this conceptual work..."

But you snuck it in on *Mishima*, too.

Well, yes, it's true, I snuck it in on **Mishima** as far as the director was concerned, but the producer always knew that that's what the film required. That's why he hired me. And it just was a matter of bringing the director up to speed.

Tom Luddy played a very important role because he got [editor Michael] Chandler, me, Philip Glass, Eiko Ishioka. He got all of those people around Paul and all of those people had such an incredible contribution. But it's always that way. Filmmaking is collaborative and that's why I find it so exciting. I don't know how well I would do if I was just out on my own, doing my own little compositions and saying: "Here world, here is my stuff." It's so much more exciting to be in the midst of many other people who have great minds and great contributions.

Philip Glass' music inspired me so much. Many of my sounds were tailored to fit within his music. I could control the pitch of the sound on my keyboard to match the key of his music. That worked out very well in certain cases. That was another advantage of having the score so much in advance. I could do stuff that wouldn't either be buried by it or try to overpower it.

On the picture *Tough Guys Don't Dance* did you find yourself tutoring Norman Mailer, who had never directed a commercial picture before?

I always had to be the voice of what was realistic though I hate being in that position because it's like the renowned physicist J. Robert Oppenheimer said [paraphrasing], "There are children on the streets who can solve my most complicated problems in physics." Just because somebody doesn't know the intimate technology of film doesn't mean that they can't stumble onto an exciting idea. Norman, a lot of times, would come up with really good ideas—they would sound stupid, they would sound difficult, they would sound impossible, but I would do them and they would turn out to be great.

For example, Norman had a thing about punches and about guns. When we came to create the punching effects for the fight scene he said, "Hey, I'm a fighter—I know what a punch should sound like. Why don't I sit here and hit myself?"

(Laughter, guffaw)

That was my reaction, too. I said, "Norman, you can do that if you want but I have these perfectly good punches that we can use." And he listened to them and he said, "No, those don't sound like what a punch should sound like."

So he ended up sitting here hitting himself and recording it and bit by bit it started to come together and I started to manipulate the sounds a bit and began to think, "Well, maybe we've got something a bit different here," and it worked.

Where did he hit himself?

He hit himself everywhere: in the jaw, in the chest; he really went for it. That's what I liked about Norman: he threw himself into everything he was doing.

10
Star Trek IV: The Voyage Home
Sound effects editing

Mark Mangini

At the time of his Oscar nomination for Best Sound Effects editing for **Star Trek IV: The Voyage Home**, 11-year sound veteran Mark Mangini discussed how he had mixed synthetic sound sources with those produced by a live improvisational jazz musician to produce the complex other-worldly "probe" sound around which so much of the **STIV** action revolves.

Precis

*How the **STIV** whale sounds (probe vocalizations) were created, starting with whale song, experimentation with saxophones, didjeridus, speeding up and layering and gating of whale song, use of rare Roger Paine whale song recordings and notch filters to remove whale feeding sounds (krill), multitrack recording through eight channels of pitch change mixed to 2-channel stereo master, improvisational (multiphonic) jazz addition to mix.*

Mark Mangini's credits

Star Trek, the Motion Picture (1979)
Raiders of the Lost Ark (1981) Steven Spielberg
Under Fire (1983) Roger Spottiswoode
Amazing Stories (1985-6) (Steven Spielberg TV series)
Star Trek IV: The Voyage Home (1986) Leonard
  Nimoy
Innerspace (1987) Joe Dante
Robocops II (1990) Irving Kershner
All I Want for Christmas (1991) Robert Lieberman
Kafka (1991) Steven Soderbergh
Aladdin (1992) Jon Musker and Ron Clements
Bram Stoker's Dracula (1992) Francis Coppola
Newsies (1992) Kenny Ortega
Cool Running (1993) Jon Turteltaub
The Discoverers (1993) Greg MacGillivray
Matinee (1993) Joe Dante
Son of the Pink Panther (1993) Blake Edwards
Look Who's Talking Now (1993) Tom Ropelewski
Neil Simon's Lost in Yonkers (1993) Martha Coolidge
Rudy (1993) David Anspaugh
Suture (1994) Scott McGehee and David Siegel
Robert A. Heinlein's The Puppet Masters (1994)
  Stuart Orme
The Flintstones (1994) Bryan Levant
The Lion King (1994) Roger Allers
  and Rob Minkoff
Die Hard with a Vengeance (1995) Jon McTiernan
Fluke (1995) Carlo Carlei

Would you describe how you created the whales sounds in *Star Trek IV*?

The probe vocalizations all started from whale song, which was my first instinct and Leonard's [Nimoy, **STIV** director] first instinct. It seemed awfully literal at first and we tried it and didn't like our first test and threw it out and then started using things like saxophones and didjeridus [a primitive aboriginal musical instrument from Australia], which Leonard didn't like. We ended up using whale song that was sped up, then layered and severely gated so that we could remove scrimp noise—it was a rather complicated process. In order to get a good whale recording you have to usually record it while it's feeding and it usually feeds on krill, which like scrimp make a noise like a castanet, a snapping noise, that ruins just about every whale recording ever made except for two or three which Roger [Paine, preeminent whale sound recordist] has gotten.

Most whale recordings in the world have a certain amount of krill as well as water and ocean noise on them. So we had a huge problem right off the bat getting a recording that was clean enough to use in a motion picture. For scientific purposes these are great accurate recordings but for dramatic purposes they're pretty dirty. Roger had a couple which sounded as if he had brought a humpback whale into an ADR stage.

So some of the best whale performances have a lot of krill on them so we had to very heavily gate them. Then after it was gated we double notch filtered it with one of those UREI Little Dippers. In between the vocalizations we could clean out all the crud, then during the vocalizations we had the UREI working to try to notch filter out the krill. Then it went into an AMS pitch changer and on a multitrack recorder we would layer harmonic intervals of the original whale vocalization.

So let's say on track one of the multitrack was the whale vocalization at its normal pitch. On track two we would pitch it up, let's say, a minor third, on track three we would pitch it yet again a major fifth, all the way up to eight channels of pitch change. So we had eight voices generated from the one recording on top of each other so it was a multiphonic, if you will, vocalization.

That 8-channel element was then mixed down to a 2-channel stereo master. Then on top of that we had this fellow Vinnie Golia, who's this bizarre jazz saxophonist, woodwind performer, come in and listen to the material that we had made from whale vocalizations. And with contra bass saxophones and bass saxophones and all these bizarre instruments that he's got, we had him perform his version of whale song, looping the whale with these instruments. He does some incredibly amazing stuff with saxophones and other woodwind instruments such as getting multiphonics out of these instruments; he even got a pretty darn good whale song right out of his sax, which blended very nicely with what we were doing.

So we added Vinnie's elements to the whale song; a lot of it was like squeaking and squawking—it wasn't musical: he was trying to make a sound effect. Then we harmonized that yet again with another layer of upper harmonics, then passed it through a graphic equalizer to tone it down—it got very screechy and shrill. And that was pretty much the probe vocalizations: the questions [asked of the time-bound whales].

How did the jazz musician get involved?

That was my idea. John Postisil [another of the sound effects editors] and I were sitting around the studio one day—this was before Leonard showed up—struggling to come up with an idea for the probe sound. We were thinking of using musical instruments for the sound and asked ourselves what kinds of instruments could be evocative and sound vocal and have a certain depth (or bass) to them.

The probe is supposed to be huge, the size of a planet. We decided that a saxophone might be an interesting place to start. We experimented with some tracks produced by an amateur saxophonist: we slowed them down then sped them up. They were interesting and that got us thinking that if we would get an accomplished saxophonist who had a good deal of control we'd have something to work with.

We turned up Vinnie Golia who told us about this approach he uses to playing called multiphonics, where he can get two or even three notes out of a sax at one time; he can get three pitches out of one blow without moving his fingers. We sent Vinnie some tapes of whale songs so he could practice imitating them. He also brought in a didjeridu, it's a giant long pipe made out of a hollowed-out branch. It takes a very well defined blowing technique to get any sound out of it at all because the aperture you blow in is about three inches wide. It makes this weird fog-horn like noise. We used the didjeridu at the end of the picture when it's [the probe] chatting with the whales. We added that to the layered sound I talked about before.

11
Explorers
Sound effects editing

Mike Minkler

As a teenager Mike Minkler swept floors at his father's Hollywood Independent Sound Service company. After a seven-year apprenticeship there, he was promoted to studio work at Warner Bros. In the 1970s he became part owner of Lion's Gate, where he experimented a good deal in designing film sound tracks. "I love just playing; I was also developing my own creative tastes. There were times when I'd have over 50 pieces of outboard equipment going all at the same time for processing—using, for example, flanges and delay lines. That was fun but I have found that I get better tracks these days given to me by the sound editor, and also my tastes have gone back to a tighter more precise, simpler mix than the wild crazy gimmicky type mix."

Mike Minkler has won the British Academy Award for Best Sound for his work as rerecording mixer on **Star Wars** (1977) and the MPSE award for Best Sound Effects for **Wolfen** (1981) (supervising rerecording mixer). He has also been nominated for four American Academy awards for Best Sound: **Electric Horseman** (effects rerecording mixer) (1979), **Altered States** (1980) (effects rerecording mixer), **Tron** (1982) (supervising rerecording mixer), and **Chorus Line** (1985) (music rerecording mixer). In his 17 years in filmmaking he has participated in the mixing of more than 87 feature films.

Mike Minkler's credits

Star Wars (1977) George Lucas
Electric Horseman (1979) Sydney Pollack
Altered States (1980) Ken Russell
Wolfen (1981) Michael Wadleigh
Tron (1982) Steven Lisberger
Explorers (1985) Joe Dante
A Chorus Line (1985) Richard Attenborough
The Addams Family (1991) Barry Sonnenfeld
Bill and Ted's Bogus Journey (1991) Pete Hewitt
The Doors (1991) Oliver Stone
The Indian Runner (1991) Sean Penn
JFK (1991) Oliver Stone
Little Man Tate (1991) Jody Foster
Pastime (1991) Robin B. Armstrong
Hoffa (1992) Danny Devito
Lovefield (1992) Jonathan Kaplan
Pure Country (1992) Christopher Cain
Sommersby (1993) Jon Amiel
Last Action Hero (1993) Jon McTiernan
Heaven and Earth (1993) Oliver Stone
Cliff Hanger (1993) Renny Harlin
American Heart (1993) Martin Bell
Deception (1993) Graeme Clifford
The Getaway (1994) Roger Donaldson
Natural Born Killers (1994) Oliver Stone
Next Karate Kid (1994) Christopher Cain
That's Entertainment III (1994) Bud Friedgen and
    Michael J. Sheridan
True Lies (1994) James Cameron
Cutthroat Island (1995) Reny Harlin
Die Hard with a Vengeance (1995) Jon McTiernan
Judge Dredd (1995) Danny Cannon
Moonlight and Valentino (1995) David Anspaugh
Showgirls (1995) Paul Verhoeven

Precis

*Most impressive recent use of hardware on feature **Explorers**—dozens of effects created on Lexicon and Lark systems, started with organic original material--footsteps and belt buckle sounds, also used Aphex compressor/expander, used to solve dialogue rerecording problems, early use of digital in post.*

How has your hardware changed in recent years?

It's changed a bit. What I use these days more than anything else is a Lexicon 224XL LARC, which I feel is the finest digital reverb device made. It's just amazing what you can do with it: a lot of people who have made them just use them for one or two functions.

What was your most impressive use of that hardware in recent times?

Probably on **Explorers**, where kids met aliens and went up into a spaceship. We had to create different acoustic environments for the different rooms of the ship. I had to create dozens of effects with the Lexicon. For example, the kids went flying through a tube for which we wanted to create the sound of the squealing of their shoes and their clothing. Since we didn't know what material the tube was made out of we could do anything we wanted. We came up with some unbelievable kinds of squeals and rubbing and moaning and groaning, all from that one device. And when they get to the end of the tube—what they're hearing down at the bottom of that tube were these strange kinds of echoes with slight bits

171

of rubbing and pinging going on in the background. That was all done with the Lark.

What does the Lark do that other hardware can't do?

It has a sound that's more distinct, and it's also more versatile. You can manipulate their programs or create your own programs; there must be a half-million to a million variables.

For the squealing effect what did you start with?

Footstep sounds or belt buckle sounds: organic original material. I also find the Aphex compressor/expanders very useful because of the transparency of the compression they render. They work and you cannot hear them working; and you can use them extremely subtly or very heavily and you never hear them working. You never hear the sound change or be colored at all. In contrast to all the other similar devices I work with which you can hear very distinctly—yet these other devices claim to be transparent also.

I use it for dialogue; it can take care of extremely fast, rapid transient type sounds like dialogue. The Aphex smooths it out extremely well.

Give me an example of a problem it helped you solve?

All dialogue is a problem because it's usually recorded under very adverse conditions and it's like "live out there" on the set, and location recordists often don't record a second take just because it make not have sounded that great or because someone jumped on a line. The mixer is mixing it and he doesn't know that the actors didn't do it similar to how they rehearsed it; it may be up too loud or down too soft. Well we have to live with whatever it was we get because they're not going to reshoot just for sound.

So the Aphex smooths out the raw, rugged production track like nothing else I've ever heard. It does the same thing for ADR. It takes all of those peaks and rough edges off of the track without coloring the sound.

Another significant change that's come along in the last five years is digital recording. I've done a couple of pictures digitally, though not every element on the picture was recorded digitally. We did as much as we had control of. It was a great experience.

Which elements were recorded digitally?

The production track was not because it's a risk. It was done analog. The rest of the tracks were digitally recorded.

How were you able to convince them to go digital for post production?

It was their idea. It was a Willy Nelson picture [**Red-Headed Stranger**] and he does all of his recordings digitally. There was a good deal of music in the film.

The great thing for me was that we didn't have the kinds of problems you normally have with analog, such as generation loss. I usually have to go through four or five generations before they're out the door. You also don't have a headroom problem, you don't have wow and flutter problems, you don't have signal to noise problems or cross talk or intermodulation distortion. All of those are tremendous advantages. They're subtle but if you add those up—wow!

Do those efficiencies show up in the budget?

173

Probably not. If you could rent a digital setup for the same price as an analog setup, I'd say it could show up in the budget because you never have to go back and do anything over again because, for example, the track's fallen apart, which happens on analog.

12
Beatrice
the director/composer collaboration

Bertrand Tavernier

Though he is best known for his exquisite visual imagination and provocative film subjects, French director Bertrand Tavernier regards the creation of music tracks to be a vital part of the filmmaking process. As he showed in his beautiful, impressionistic **A Sunday in the Country** (1983) and his jazz homage **Round Midnight** (1985), Tavernier has an acute sense of how to use music to color the moods of his films. As a rule, he starts to take notes on musical concepts for his films during the screenwriting phase of pre-production—well before the composer generally joins the creative team. "For me, the music is not an illustration of the film," he says. "It's dreaming around the film."

Tavernier's film **Beatrice** is a realistic tale of a mad, defeated medieval lord who tyrannizes his wife, son, daughter (Beatrice) and castle subjects. Because of its stark depiction of incest and generally bleak tone **Beatrice** has stirred considerable controversy. Yet the film is never exploitative, and at its heart is a film about faith and spiritual crisis, not the rigors of life in the Middle Ages.

For the haunting, occasionally abstract music that accompanies the film's striking visuals, Tavernier hired jazz bassist/composer Ron Carter, who had appeared as a musician in **Round Midnight**. To get a sense of the story, Carter (who has played music with everyone from Miles Davis to Wes Montgomery to Sonny Rollins) read an early draft of the script of **Beatrice**, "But I was a little embarrassed because it's really kind of out there for me," the soft-spoken musician says. "I'm a lot more conservative than that." Next, he did a tremendous amount of book and interview research into commonly used musical instruments of the period (sackbutt, viele, hurdy-gurdy, recorders) so that he could use them throughout the 48 minutes of music the film needed. On top of that, he wrote some typically inspired music for the bass, and also used an early 20th-century art song by Lily Boulanger called "PieJesu" as a jumping-off point for some of his original music. (That song, a favorite of Tavernier's for years, also appears in the film).

Both Tavernier and Carter were interviewed about the film and its music.

Precis

Tavernier's intention to present a direct experience of Medieval life, the function of modern music in a period film, recording and mixing of the track.

Bertrand Tavernier's credits

The Watchmaker of St. Paul (1974)
Que la Fête Commence (1975)
The Judge and the Assassin (1976)
Spoiled Children (1977)
Death Watch (1980)
Coup de Torchon (1982)
A Week's Vacation (1982)
Mississippi Blues (1983)
Sunday in the Country (1984)

Round Midnight (1986)
Beatrice (1987)
Life and Nothing But (1989)
Daddy Nostalgia (1990)
La Guerre Sans Nom (1992)
Contre L'Oubli (1992)
L.627 (1992)
La Fille De D'artagnan (1994)
L'Appat (1995)
Capitaine Cunan (1995)

Beatrice is a very brutal film....

A lot of people find it that way. For me it's a mystical film but it's brutal because the period is brutal. For the people of the time it's not brutal: when they see a woman [in the film] killing a baby in the snow, nobody reacts, because that was part of daily life. Maybe that's too difficult for a modern audience to get. An audience may need to have a go-between. But we wanted to get rid of something which is very bad in a lot of period and historical films: the fact that characters most of the time are speaking to explain things to a modern audience

However the music of *Beatrice* is modern music. Some of it reminded me of Schoenberg. Were you attempting to make the period more accessible to the audience by using modern music?

No, because it's full of percussion. I think a lot of people don't find it easy; they find it violent. When you do a film about the 18th Century, why use 18th Century music? Sometimes it's a little bit too arty or too easy. I wanted an interpretation of that kind of music. I wanted somebody who was going to dream around that music. If

I'd been very, very faithful [to the Medieval period] I'd never have used Lily Boulanger, which was [composed in] 1918, and who composed something which was closer to [Gabriel] Faure than to the religious music of the period. It might have been more accessible maybe if I had used the music of the time because it's a very lyrical, easy, beautiful music. I wanted music which was going to fit the feeling of the character and the theme. For me, the music is not an illustration of the film; it's dreaming around the film. I'm very proud of Ron's work. It's something which is quite new and quite interesting; which is again proving that the jazz musician can do things which are beyond his range.

Is part of the purpose of the music to convey the spirituality of the Medieval period?

Yes, of course. And I don't know if Ron is religious, we never spoke of that. But I think he got that immediately in the movie, and he got the beauty of Beatrice.

Why did use you modern music to contrast with a very realistic, Medieval story?

I don't know. I don't think the film is only a period film and maybe that's why I use that music. It's as if Ron was building a bridge and telling the audience that this is not only a story about a girl in the 14th Century, it's a story about the human soul today.

How much of the music and dialogue were recorded live?

Whenever you see musicians performing in the film, they were recorded live. I love to record live on the set because very often in a film you can see that the musicians, when they are dubbed or post-synched, they don't play the note you're hearing. So whenever I have musicians in the image I always record live.

About ninety-five percent of the dialogue was recorded live. In addition we added many effects. For instance, my sound engineer, Michel Desrois, got about 50 different kinds of winds in that castle where we were shooting. So we sometimes mixed different kinds of winds with the winds we had already on the live sound track. Desrois' god is Jim Webb, who worked with Robert Altman at Lion's Gate. He likes to record more than one track at a time while shooting on the set. It's as if he was mixing during the shooting. Desrois would love to have 18 tracks on the set at one time.

Was *Beatrice* mixed in Paris?

Yes, like **Round Midnight**. I try to work a lot on the sound. I love to work on the sound—to get sound which is live, brutal and violent. We added a lot of things to the original sound track that's part of the 5% or 10% [not recorded during filming]: all of the birds and dogs. We were not pleased with the sounds of the dogs and birds that we had, which were recorded in France. We decided that there were many more rapacious sounding birds during the Middle Ages; so we used all the bird sounds which we recorded when we were doing **Coup de Torchon** in Senegal. The African birds and dogs make much more violent sounds.

Composer Ron Carter
On creating the score for *Beatrice*

Precis

Function that music plays in **Beatrice**, *criteria used to choose scenes to orchestrate.*

Did you participate in the recording of the score in Paris?

Yes, they wanted to receive the score before I got there, so I sent it a week before I arrived so the musicians could practice their parts. On the day I arrived in Paris I got there at 9:30 in the morning and we started recording the music at 11:00. By 7:00 we had recorded all but three cues.

This was synched to the picture?

No, all timed. They put it to the picture after I left.

Was there any significant change from the time of your recording until the final mix?

I made some wild percussion sounds at random: two seconds of wind chimes, three seconds of wood block, five seconds of cymbals. Other than one change the final score was just as Tavernier and I had discussed it at the viewing of the rough cut.

Did you participate in the mix?

No. When I left Paris, I left knowing I had recorded all the music I had written.

How did you take notes during the screening of the rough cut?

I had a notebook, a very small flashlight and a stop watch. I would make notations: girl near tree, start the stop watch, and stop it where I thought the scene stopped, ten seconds. My notation would be: wind chimes and alto flute. And I would do that for each of the cues in the rough cut.

How did you decide which scenes you wanted to put music under?

Just how they struck me in the movie. Tavernier didn't suggest where the music should go. For example, the opening scene shows soldiers going off to war: a very majestic scene, where a priest blesses the soldiers. So I indicated a sackbutt, alto recorder, percussion and string bass to give a full sound with this very open air and only four or five instruments. I make that decision then when I see the picture for the first time. I don't see it three or four times to come up with different points of view; I trust my instinct. My view is that the music was never intended to be the dominant element in the movie; the music was intended to always underpin or underscore or enhance in some form or fashion—perhaps in direct contrast to the image. When the father's chasing the son, during that scene I used some sparse percussion. It could have

181

been done a lot of ways, perhaps, but it seemed to me given the open air and the various cuts from the horses and the riders and the son stumbling through the bush, some kind of sparse and varied percussion sound would enhance this level of anxiety and tension. So rather than use long notes I used some small percussive sounds to give this different texture to each image on the screen.

How did you distinguish between scenes that you felt needed music and others you felt didn't need music?

This wasn't a romantic picture, per se. So right away I discount any kind of lush, multi-harmonic, emotional sound. That was totally out of the question based on the script I had read. So with the mentality of the 14th Century and the limited instruments that were available to them at that time, I have to look for scenes that not only demand music but demand music with these limited instruments. These instruments couldn't play many notes because they were monochromatic: you couldn't play thirds and fourths at one time, because they weren't to that stage of development yet. I also didn't want to get involved in overdubbing because that wasn't the sound of the time being portrayed in the movie.

How would you compare the task of composing for a jazz ensemble and composing for an ensemble of medieval musical instruments?

The difference is with a jazz score you don't need to write so much because good jazz players have a sense of what you want. And because the language itself is so nebulous—it's hard to write a real jazz phrase because of the inflections that are really difficult to notate rhythmically—most jazz players will sense what the phrase will sound like and will interpret it for you. It takes a lot of weight off the composer to write specifically what he wants because guys will interpret for him what he wants.

Are you saying it's a lot easier to compose a jazz score?

Oh, yeah, there's nothing to that, man. I do it every night when I make the gigs.

13
Foreigns
Preparing music and effects

Foreigns aren't what they should be. European audiences prefer dubbed versions of foreign features while American audiences would rather see subtitled ones.

Despite near-record export revenues of $1.44 billion (**Daily Variety**) in a recent year from the U.S. many European dubbers believe Hollywood neglects the needs of Continental audiences for quality dubs of major studio feature films.

The general stateside practice is for rerecording mixers to prepare the M+E (music and effects) at the end of the mix and send it to Europe with the domestic English-language version as well as a transcription of the dialogue. But many things can go wrong before audiences get to hear the track in their local versions. (German, Spanish, Italian, and French dubs are common, while a boffo feature, such as Disney's **Aladdin** was dubbed into 22 languages.)

The M+E is usually prepared by the effects editors, who know where to find the holes caused by removal of the domestic dialogue track. When it leaves the studio the M+E takes the form of a 35 mm. full-coat with four discrete tracks of music and effects. Track 1 has left music and left effects; track 2 is center music and center effects; track 3 is right music and right effects; and track 4 contains surround music and surround effects. These discrete tracks are mixed so as to allow the stateside mixer maximum control. A mono string of the domestic dialogue track on separate mag is also sent.

One important difference between the M+E tracks prepared for the domestic composite and the foreign version, is that the latter has sweeteners added into its mix to fill the holes left by removal of the domestic dialogue track.

Though most foreigns are made without a director's representative present at the European site, those that do receive a rep's attention not unexpectedly tend to be the more carefully manicured and well-heeled productions, such as **Toys, Bugsy,** and **Avalon** (Barry Levinson), **Godfather III** and **Bram Stoker's Dracula** (Francis Coppola). Sound designer Richard Beggs, who was the on-site director's rep on all of these except **Dracula**, emphasizes the importance of the foreigns contract. Whether or not a rep is present, he notes, the efficacy of the foreigns mix starts with the contract between the stateside studio and the European distributor under whose terms the studio promises to supply the distributor with a completely filled track. This is loosely defined as two-thirds of the sound elements of the track, the M+E part. The other third, which the foreign distributor must provide, is the foreign language dialogue track.

The presence of the director's rep on the foreigns mix can go a long way toward alleviating many of the creative problems that arise. Not surprisingly, European mixers and audiences expect the same high quality tracks Hollywood supplies stateside. In fact, the domestic is often thought of as the god that must be worshipped under any and all circumstances. Beggs encountered the consequences of this blind devotion on **Bugsy** when Barry Levinson decided to use on the domestic a less-than-perfect dialogue recording of a superbly acted scene. The setting is Annette Bening's house when she and Warren Beatty have just finished watching the gangster's home movies. "The original production track was extremely noisy and trashy-sounding, but we had to use it because the performances were fantastic, and there was no way we could duplicate them with looping. We made the production track sound as good as we could to save the dialogue but it's still noisier than we would have liked."

Oddly enough, when the Europeans heard the domestic in the course of making their foreign-language tracks, they insisted on slavishly imitating the noisy domestic dialogue track. "In the foreign we didn't put in the same amount of noise that was in the domestic, because now I could make it the way I and the director wanted it to be," Beggs recalls. "We put in the kind of [quiet] background we would have liked to have had in the first place."

Continental mixers also feel under the gun from their bosses, the European distributors, to adhere to the domestic. And they often feel that they have no other way to know the director's original intention. In a reversal of what often happens to Hollywood pictures abroad, on **Bugsy** Levinson and Beggs were able to come closer to their original artistic intention in the foreign—with a clean dialogue track—than they were in the domestic.

With consultants in every major European country, Dolby Sound Laboratories plays a significant role in assuring some degree of quality control in the making of foreigns, working closely with local distributors. One of Dolby's more seasoned hands in this area is senior European consultant Ray Gillon, who has worked on over 400 films. Gillon outlines some of the factors that affect the making of foreigns: the role of distributors, music and effects, time, and translations/adaptations.

Although the M+Es received from the major studios are generally OK, Gillon has seen some remarkable exceptions, such as the 60 FXs and chunks of music absent from **Wild at Heart**, and all the music from Dolly Parton's film **Rhinestone**. In some cases such omissions can be intentional (such as the result of non-clearance of music rights), but usually it's just a case of poor communication between the studio and the foreign mixer. On **Rhinestone** the multitalented Gillon took the direct approach to fixing the hole: "The studio got me a guitar and I played the music; we rerecorded it there and then."

At Joinville, one of France's major studios, founding designer and technical director John Rutledge and rerecording mixer Bernard Leroux (**The Lover**) comment that about 70% of the M+Es they receive are imperfect.

"The main complaint concerns incomplete M+E tracks," remarks Rutledge. "In many films, much of the location sound has been conserved, which is fine, provided that atmospheres and footsteps during dialogue sequences are rerecorded afterwards for the M+E track. If this is not done then those sounds will not be available for the foreign mix, and the engineer will have to find something in a sound library."

Though some Hollywood features gross more abroad than domestically, studios are fairly consistent in allotting fixed budgets of two to four days, with flexibility only in the number of hours worked per day; in Germany a difficult picture like **JFK** took 80 hours to do, while **Home Alone** was whipped out in seven hours. This variability was a direct function of both the complexity of the mix for each and the budget available to do each job.

Under these restricted working conditions time spent fixing an incomplete M+E takes away from precious dialogue recording time. The Europeans try to make up for such limitations by passing along reports of problems to mixers in other countries next in line to do the foreign.

Another source of possible headaches is the all important translations, which in Gillon's view, should always be done by a native speaker. The drawback is that they may not be **au fait** with modern slang, which changes rapidly. Translations should be read back into English and compared with the original; this will likely bring problems to light quickly and help avoid costly retakes.

One of Beggs more memorable headaches occurred on the **Bugsy** German foreigns mix, at the nostalgic scene when Meyer Lansky (Ben Kingsley) says to a fellow hoodlum, "Remember when we used to hold up kids playing craps in the street?"

It comes out in German, "Remember when we used to knock over the kids playing with shit in the street?" When Beggs asked about this unusual translation his German mixer said it sounded strange to him but thought it might have been vernacular for the period.

It is often the case that the American word has three syllables whereas it's German equivalent has eight. The only choice, says Beggs, is to change the conversation, to adapt rather than translate literally. However, if that word contains a crucial plot point, you're out of luck.

Since most non-English-language features shot in Europe never get shown outside their country of origin, Continental producers have lately shown increasing interest in shooting in English for the most lucrative single-language global market. Last year's U.S. box office success of the French production **The Lover** proved the viability of such an approach. Director J.J. Annaud (**The Bear**) shot a guide track in English in Vietnam, where moped background sounds were all but overpowering. This combination of language and locale allowed him to take advantage of the ambience and local color so central to the Marguerite Duras novel, and still record in the language that would prove the biggest market for the film. Although English-language track looping was recorded in London, rerecording mixers at Joinville found themselves in the unusual position of creating a foreign in French for domestic release.

The commercialism of the production was also reflected in the variety of other foreigns created: Spanish, German, Italian, Thai, and Japanese as well as TV versions in a number of Eastern European languages. **The Lover** went on to win the highly regarded Golden Reel Award for the quality of its soundtrack.

Other pictures mixed this way at Joinville include **Vincent and Theo** (Robert Altman), **The Mahabharata** (Peter Brook), **Bitter Moon** (Roman Polanski), and **Salaam Bombay** (Meera Nair).

Although the most successful German export dub, **The Boat**, was shot in German and later dubbed into English, Toni Ketterle, head of Bavaria FilmSound, reports that it is his facility's practice to record features set for international release in English, later making a German domestic dub, such as **Homo Faber** (Volker Schlöndorff), **Cement Garden** (Andrew Birkin) and **In the Name of the Rose** (J.J. Annaud).

European and American mixers agree that education and better communication between mixers (Continental and stateside) and distributors will go a long way toward alleviating many of the obstacles that get in the way of achieving their common goal: a track that both serves the film audience and faithfully represents the director's original artistic intent.

14
Othello, Lawrence of Arabia
restoring ailing tracks

Fueled by robust laser disk sales and advances in home video and cable nearfield sound-delivery systems, feature film distributors no longer confine their restoration work to pictures. Instead they are increasingly recognizing the ancillary market value offered through the highest possible sound quality. Distributors such as Columbia Pictures, Castle Films and United Artists have collaborated with veteran editors and innovative audio restoration teams to bring back from their archives and likely oblivion the likes of Orson Welles'**Othello, Lawrence of Arabia** from David Lean, and John Schlesinger's **Midnight Cowboy**, to name but three.

Before the advent of widespread magnetic recording in the early 1950s, virtually all Hollywood feature soundtracks were recorded optically. As a result, when distributors wish to obtain the best original sound from a venerable picture today they must go back to an optical negative. Traditionally, optical tracks are read with photocells such as are used in movie theater projectors (or on a Rank-Cintel), a method which gives a rough reading, seeing scratches and dirt as noise. A processing system originally developed to make the pioneering quintophonic sound track for the Who rock opera **Tommy** (1975), is used today by Chace Productions to restore damaged optical negative tracks of treasured Hollywood features. According to Chace president Bob Heiber, COSP's one-line video camera process knows an audio signal when it sees one, clearly distinguishing between original blacks, clear track areas and the extraneous accumulations of time and neglect normally played back as noise. Chace's one-line camera is a CCD (charge coupled device) that does not scan as do conventional video cameras.

Heiber is especially proud of a series of foreign-feature restorations that Chace saw through to Dolby stereo theatrical release.

"We had the German optical negative soundtrack," he recalls, "which was a composite, and through the use of the negative optical reader [COSP] NoNoise, and the Chace Surround Sound system for programming it, along with a beautifully restored LCRS music and effects track that Disney did, we mixed all those components together, cleaned it up and created a German 35 mm. stereo release soundtrack."

Chace also successfully carried out the quarter-century rejuvenation of **Midnight Cowboy**, using one of their proprietary systems. Heiber's mixers started with a monaural dialogue, music, and effects stem and the stereo music score for Fred Neil's **Everybody's Talkin'**. Using the Chace Stereo Surround system their mixers turned these tracks into left, center, right, and surround for each track: dialogue, music, and effects. Mike Minkler at Skywalker South then re-matrixed these tracks into Dolby left total, right total, for theatrical release.

Until its recent restoration it was always a sad experience to hear the badly flawed **Othello** (1952) dialogue track from the same director who gave us the illustrious track to **Citizen Kane**. As part of Castle Pictures' elaborate restoration of one of only three Welles Shakespeare films Magno Sound and Video was hired to restore the picture's badly muffled track. Magno used an approach that harkened back to the wellsprings of optical sound. Starting with a 35 mm. optical negative print, audio department head Rick Nicholas confirmed with a densitometer and microscope that the variable area track had been too densely printed. Observes Nicholas: "If the track is not printed densely enough, it will produce a lot of noise and distortion. If it's printed too dark, a muffled quality and sibilant distortion will result."

To restore the track to optimum condition Nicholas conducted a series of trial-and-error cross modulation tests working closely with his lab, LabLink.

"We instructed our lab to record onto a 35 mm. optical negative track a high-frequency tone with a low-band carrier at a variety of lamp currents," he explains, "which gave us different densities. On correctly printed black-and-white pictures the optical track should be gray; on color film the optical track should be magenta."

If the lab is shooting the lamp too hot, the optical soundtrack will print too densely, sounding muffled and losing the high frequencies. Printing on polyester film the normal range is 1.15 to 1.20, measuring the darkness of the track as read by a densitometer. The range from clear transparency to solid black is 0.026 to 3.00.

Because of the photographic nature of the sound transfer an additional critical loss must be worked into the process.

Comments Nicholas: "When we shoot a 35 mm. optical negative we add EQ or film loss equalization to that negative. And we do that because when we marry the negative soundtrack and the negative picture together to come out with a positive image, there is a generational loss. To compensate for this loss we pre-emphasize the high frequencies; in the making of the positive print this loss is accounted for. Our cross-modulation tests tell us how much to skew this pre-emphasis."

In all about 30 cross-modulation tests throughout the length of **Othello** were made. Working on one reel at a time, he singled out troublesome sections, listened to each test for the best sound quality then transferred these to a

193

Sonic Solutions No-Noise workstation, where clicks, hiss, and pops were removed

Back in the 1960s and 1970s David Lean's **Lawrence of Arabia** was released in no fewer than four versions—a full length road-show version, a shorter, widely released theatrical version, a few years later another shorter theatrical version, and finally, shortest of all, a television version.

A quarter-century later **Lawrence's** restoration was overseen by Robert Harris, who had restored Abel Gance's **Napoleon**, and Tom Payton, who worked closely with director Lean and picture editor Anne V. Coates. The result was a director's cut, which differed only slightly from the road-show release. At which point sound editor Richard Anderson was hired to restore the often sketchy sound track.

Oscar winner Anderson, whose credit is usually supervising sound editor, has worked on more than forty theatrical features. In toiling on his first restoration this editor found he had to call on all of his quarter of a century's experience to solve the wide array of unpredictable editorial problems posed by **Lawrence of Arabia's** crippled track. Some knowledge of film history came in handy as well.

Anderson began with the only full version of the track that existed, a 6-track master of the shortest version for TV. In addition, some sound elements existed of picture scenes that had been cut out.

Recalls Anderson: "It was like trying to put together a jigsaw puzzle where a number of the pieces were missing. We had all the picture but had large holes in the sound tracks. We also had an M+E (music and effects) track for some of the scenes."

In one such scene a powerful Sheik (Anthony Quinn) invites his guests to dine with him in his desert dwelling. The TV version showed the Sheik in his tent dining with a group of tribesmen, who are fearful of the Sheik for no apparent reason. The road-show version showed tribesmen arriving at the Sheik's camp amidst the fanfare of a powerful army of hundreds of soldiers, horses, and tents. In the TV version the motivation for the tribesmen's fear was absent, leaving the audience baffled. The restored version made the scene dramatically whole again by putting back shots of the Sheik's powerful army.

Fortunately this scene didn't contain dialogue, just music and an effects track of horses and gunfire; as it happened, by having the M+E Anderson had the elements he needed to reconstruct the scene.

At other times track could just be found in the form of a 35 mm. mono composite optical track. Here the only solution was to collapse the track down to mono, which brought its own issues.

"We had the problem of the optical being ahead of the picture by 20 frames. Whenever we removed a picture scene we were removing track from the previous picture scene. When they made the shortened [TV] version they had all the sub-elements so they remixed it, so you didn't hear the incoming next scene that had been eliminated."

In those cases Anderson had a hole which he filled in by copying from another portion of the track. Another scene in a tent had the British army officers plotting strategy against the Turkish army. Offstage we hear bagpipes playing and soldiers marching. The synch tracks for those scenes had been lost, although inexplicably outtakes still existed. "So with the aid of an original dialogue transcription we hand edited different takes to match the actor's lips. In some scenes then we were able to get dialogue from alternate takes and later added the effects in as if it were a new movie," comments Anderson.

Peter O'Toole ended up looping scenes to silent picture without the aid of a guide track; although in preparation for this work Harris hired a deaf lip reader who screened silent picture to verify that picture and original dialogue transcription matched.

During the entire two-month restoration process Anderson and his two-man crew had no original sound elements to work with. All he had was a 6 track mixed master that had dialogue, music and effects on the same piece of full coat mag film. "Whereas today we generally put dialogue in the center track unless a character is [positioned] hard left or hard right, where a special effect is desired, in **Lawrence** they had dialogue in all five front speakers, like a fat mono, though the effects and music were stereo. On a graph the center speaker had the most level, but somewhat mysteriously there was reverb and decay that went out to the sides.

"I thought this would be easy. I'll specify in copying the track the center channel not be copied, so when I had to extend scenes I would be able to just lay it in. It didn't appear to be like the early days of stereo where characters were panned as they moved from left to right.

"And if there was music in a scene it was also mixed with effects. So the problem I had was that whenever I had to extend music or effects everything was mixed together. In some scenes I was able to find bits of music where no one was talking or the effects weren't that prominent, and I had to loop the music to get enough footage to extend those sections."

In one scene Lawrence—wearing his bedouin robes—meets with General Allenby after returning from a trek in the desert. He has had a difficult time in the desert, where he's lost one of his assistants. For the first time the other officers, who previously thought of Lawrence as a fool, see him as a hero. The opening and closing sections of this scene are rolling shots down the halls of British headquarters with music under them, but in the middle section there was no music, just picture.

Concludes Anderson, "It was easy to fill in footsteps but I needed to not only fill in the music but have it make sense on both ends because the music was tied to the dialogue. Fortunately I was able to find a few bars of this martial marching music, loop it and get enough footage to make it match. And picture editor Coates was gracious enough to trim the scene by a few frames such that the beat of the music piece I had would match the beat of the pieces on each end.

"Today 70 mm. is mainly the Dolby format of having three full-frequency speakers across the front and two boom channels. So we reshaped the original mix in order to fit into the Dolby format to be compatible with today's common release format."

15
Open Media Framework Interchange (OMFI): global audio standardization for multimedia

"It's like the national need for a health care system. The fact that we don't have common file samples among digital audio work stations (DAWs) is an absolute hell," says Steve Shirtz, facilities manager at the Saul Zaentz Film Center.

Weddington Productions Inc. president Mark Mangini believes much of the growth in the facilities industry is being held up because of the lack of a DAW compatibility standard.

"I think the Open Media Framework Interchange (OMFI) will encourage and spur the proliferation of more workstations in my business. There are a lot of people, myself included, who are afraid to buy what will [turn out to] be a white elephant because of file incompatibility. When file formats become standardized it means that the dubbing stages will start to install playback units of workstations such that regardless of what I'm cutting on I can bring my material to the stage in a digital format to play on [such currently incompatible DAWs as] Waveframe, Pro Tools or Sonic Solutions. This will force the sound editorial houses to purchase more of them, which increases purchases and sales, which lowers costs, and increases competition. It's good for everybody."

Shirtz's extensive MO effects library used to be in AIFF and SD2 formats. At the time Pro Tools did not support AIFF so he converted his whole library to SD2. When Digidesign announced a Pro Tools upgrade which reads and writes AIFF files, Shirtz was left with the feeling he had wasted a lot of work. Nonetheless he still has to go through file translators to import his MO effects library

199

into their Sonic Solutions DAWs, which don't read AIFF, the kind of conundrum facilities cope with daily .

The cry for a global digital audio standard of compatibility has reached fever pitch in recent years primarily for two reasons: proliferation of often incompatible DAWs, running on Macintosh, Silicon Graphics and proprietary platforms, and a growing reliance on and realization of the limits of DAT, which provides a quality signal but no handles such as immediate access to dB levels.

While users see a clear need for a universal multimedia standard, manufacturers often lag behind. "Manufacturers have traditionally been suspicious of file compatibility, which they have viewed as a potential threat. Few companies have been forthcoming in promoting a common interchange format," says editor/writer/DAW designer Thomas A. Ohanian in his excellent comprehensive tome **Digital Nonlinear Editing** (Focal Press, 1993). The visionaries at Avid Technologies are an exception to that rule. In 1992 they had the foresight and enlightened self-interest to embark upon an OMFI partners program, which quickly grew to include 130 media and computer companies, 13 of which are audio developers or DAW makers. By early '93 the OMF Interchange Specification, version 1.0, was in the hands of developers at partners companies and beta testing of de jure multimedia standards was underway.

During the years DAWs have developed sans ubiquitous digital compatibility standards, mixing studios have had to make do with two crutches that pass for communication and cataloguing standards, holdovers from a withering, sluggish linear era.

From film we have pilotone (aka 60-cycle pulse).

From video we have SMPTE time code: drop and non-drop frame.

Originally designed for linear video editing, CMX

EDL's are severely limited by the fact that not all DAWs will read or write them. Those that do are restricted to in/out points for source, destination, and four possible audio channels with a fourth field available for comments. Though the perennial and far more slavish SMPTE time code does not suffer from CMX's compatibility problems its use remains largely limited to synch and production dialogue autoconforming.

The first public demonstration of OMFI occurred at AES '93 when four track cuts only and cross faded audio files were exchanged between a Dyaxis II and an Audiovision. Both DAWs displayed dB levels on their graphic interfaces and first hand accounts indicate the premier came off without a hitch. The Dyaxis II screen clearly showed beginning and end points for cross fades; a de facto time code window. Both Dyaxis and Audiovision can import and export OMFI audio files.

Studer Editec senior software engineer Lee Ann Heringer noted "We [Studer Editec and Avid] previously had our own native file formats, which were incompatible with each other." In addition, prior to AES, Avid product engineer Fady Lamaa has successfully imported and exported OMFI audio files from a Silicon Graphics (Iris Indigo series) workstation, a Macintosh Quadra/Avid Media Composer, and a Gateway 2000 PC. This in-house demonstration was performed via an ethernet connecting all three computers.

All OMFI files have two components: compositions and physical sources of media data. In audio files, compositions are edit decision lists, while media data is the audio itself. Avid supplies developers at partners companies with an OMFI Tool Kit to adapt their software to meet OMFI specs. Also central to OMFI's future is the choice of a common medium of exchange. Most likely candidates are 8 mm. Xybite tape, optical media such as MOs or networks.

Concludes AVID's Greg Clukey, "OMFI to be wildly successful requires that we have some common ways to exchange audio such as adoption of MO's. Choosing it will probably not impact the OMFI format spec. but it will affect our practical use of it.

"I would like to see all multimedia networks—LAN, WAN, and ATM—make OMFI the default file format by which applications are exchanging digital media. Network use will be a catalyst for the growth of OMFI, no doubt about it. And the reason is because it will enable more people to exchange multimedia information, something that's difficult today because it involves a lot of data. Networks today such as ethernet just can't handle that amount of data; they just don't have the bandwidth in enough time—it takes too long because it's too slow."

Appendix

The production side of *Tucker*

    Vittorio Storaro's cinematography
    Dean Tavoularis' production design

Glossary
Further reading
Index
(Order form)

Two **Tucker** production stories are included here to provide a more rounded view—however indirectly—of the relationship between a picture's cinematography, production design, and sound (cf. Richard Beggs' sound interview). They are based on lengthy interviews and personal observation with longtime Coppola collaborators Vittorio Storaro and Dean Tavoularis. The author was an extra during the shooting of the car's unveiling sequence.

TUCKER: The Man and His Dream
Vittorio Storaro
Cinematography

Francis Coppola's **Tucker: The Man and His Dream** is the story of Preston Tucker, a Midwestern American maverick who nearly reached the pinnacle of automobile industry in the 1940s, only to be foiled by industry and governmental opposition. His life was one of monumental vision and risk, and to embody that dynamism in the film, cinematographer Vittorio Storaro drew upon the style of the Italian Futurist painters.

To capture the flavor of Midwestern American life, Storaro turned to the art of Grandma Moses and Norman Rockwell. There he found metaphors for visual elements "tied to the ground: family, house, country—very naturalistic but very rich in color, like primitive paintings." He rendered these qualities "in composition and in color separation—in a kind of dynamism that is within the frame but is not part of the film.

Tucker begins at the end of World War II, when Americans are hungering for new car models. Preston Tucker (Jeff Bridges) seizes the opportunity to capture a rich new market and assembles an impressive array of auto mechanics and designers. The film traces his rise and fall, from auto salesman to near-triumph to defeat. Upon this story of personal ambition and intrigue Storaro has brought to bear a Futurist dynamism and the clean, earthy look of Midwestern popular culture.

During the quarter-century of his career, Storaro has shot more than 25 features (including six for Bernardo Bertolucci and three for Coppola), initially receiving worldwide recognition for his work with Bertolucci on

The Conformist (1971). He has shot every Bertolucci feature up to **The Little Buddha** (1994). The cinematographer's work has earned him three Academy Awards, one for **Apocalypse Now** (1979) Warren Beatty's **Reds** (1981) and Bertolucci's **The Last Emperor.**

Tucker is Francis Coppola's first collaboration with George Lucas since **American Graffiti** (1973), and more than any other single factor it may be Lucas' executive producer status that is allowing Coppola more freedom on this picture than any feature he has directed since **One from the Heart** (1982). Like **Apocalypse Now** and **One from the Heart**, Tucker teams Storaro with production designer Dean Tavoularis. (cf. accompanying chapter on Tavoularis' production design on **Tucker**).

Storaro found in the Futurist painters a way of expressing the automaker's dynamism. "Tucker is a character always in movement, "the DP explains. "The three main elements he was putting in his own car were beauty, speed and safety. Speed was one of the main elements of his life; he's always the center of a vortex of energy. The Futurist Movement mainly was concerned with how to achieve dynamism and movement in a painting, something that is not quiet but is in progress—going from one place to another."

Working closely with Coppola and Tavoularis, Storaro's visual style paralleled the picture's narrative development. "As the central conflict of Tucker's life draws near and he starts to realize his own dream, all of this energy and dynamism that was inside starts to move outside: the camera starts to move faster, the lights start to change much more than before, color starts to add in more conflict between light and shadows. The colors become much more active: yellows, oranges, reds. Colors become less saturated."

In an opening section of **Tucker**, a dealer promotional film conveys Tucker's energy, vitality and ideas as they were presented to his business associates, and serves as a contrast to the real-life scenes of Tucker's life. "This section is more airy, full of bright light and the color of the future: blues, greens, violets. Here a shift is made into an atmosphere at once less material and more angelic."

As governmental and other enemies move in on Tucker," everything starts to become more exaggerated. Everything starts to become claustrophobic. A kind of cage has been created around Tucker that tries to stop his dynamism, his intelligence, his invention—his renewal."

It is in this section that Storaro was most influenced by Italian Futurist painters, whose work he saw at a major retrospective of Futurist work in Venice in 1986. He was trying to "exaggerate the color and make the camera movement even more exaggerated, more bleak; make the perspective even stronger."

Storaro divides light into two types—point form (concentrated light, resulting in the sharp definition between dark and light) and multiform (a broader brush of light). It is in the relationship between them—their combination, their complementarity or conflict—that Storaro renders mood and feeling.

In peaceful scenes Storaro created "a sense of stillness" with what he calls "a kind of penumbra," where there is no conflict between light and shadows. In contrast, the active scenes were visually reinforced with strong distinctions between light and shadow. "Conflict means movement, dialogue, and is active," he says.

In the kitchen sequence, for example, Storaro uses light to visually reinforce the individual characters and their relationships. Tucker and his closest business ally, Abe Karatz (played by Martin Landau), are in the kitchen for a meeting about raising capital for the factory. Karatz expresses some reservations that Tucker will ever build his dream car.

The medium close shot has Tucker, at the left edge of the frame, softly lighted, and Karatz at the right edge, in highlight. In the foreground sits Tucker's family, bathed in strong fill light. For some minutes Tucker and Karatz exchange jibes. On the periphery of the shot stand Tucker's head mechanic and designer, in low-key shadow.

Karatz radiates the energy of the scene—in keeping with Storaro's dictum that light is energy—and is the center of Tucker's attention. His family is shown in strong fill light, reflecting his strong desire to include them in his plans. And lastly, his two dissenting assistants, whose opinions Tucker virtually ignores, are shadowy background figures.

As the sequence continues, the highlight on Karatz disappears, reflecting Tucker's own somewhat diminished enthusiasm; two diffuse shadows fall across their separate faces, leaving both characters half in soft light and suggesting their emotional ambivalence toward the deal.

Storaro has used Technovision lenses on virtually every feature film he has ever shot. He shot **Tucker** with Arriflex 35 mm. BL cameras using anamorphic (2.35:1) lenses, which, he observes, provide sharper and more detailed images with very fine depth of field and minimal chromatic aberration. Because the lens has no rubber or separation between the focal nodal point and the film gate "the image is stronger and more steady," he says. "There is no movement between the two different elements."

Storaro, as is his stateside custom, worked with a half-American, half-Italian crew, employing a significant amount of personally imported Italian lighting and grip equipment (Ianiro PAR lights and a Cinecittà Elemack dolly).

The setup was used to great effect in the sequence that depicts the introduction of the Tucker automobile. It was shot in what was once a thriving Ford assembly plant on the bayside docks of Richmond, California. The plant's high, airy interiors and mostly glass roof proved superb natural skylights, allowing Storaro to take full advantage of long summer days. Two broadly curving sections of bleacher seating about 400 extras (the sales force and investors) were set up facing a tall, curtained, semicircular stage. A dolly track was laid out perpendicular to the 180-degree stage from which Tucker would unveil his car.

A row of 40 incandescent stage lights lined the base of the inaugural stage, illuminating the sleek, ultramodern car from below. Another row of 40 incandescents formed a semicircular broad light band at the front of the stage and just below the set's ceiling. And high (perhaps 30') above the car three rings of Fresnel—8, 31 and 56 bulbs going out from the center and forming an almost heavenly crown—created a sparkle effect on the spit-polished Tucker below.

As the unveiling nears, Tuckers appears on stage and begins taunting the mixed audience of well-wishers and skeptics. They roar sighs of both approval and disenchantment. Storaro's dolly-mounted BL pulls away from a low angle close shot to a high curving shot, rolling behind and above the crowded bleachers, to reveal in long shot the shiny Tucker accelerating down the stage ramp and out the factory door.

Out front the unruly sea of faces awaits the new automobile. In extreme long shot the faces sparkle like jewels (as the Tucker itself will momentarily) with high key light, reflecting the source of Tucker's anxiety and energy.

Tucker's oldest son commutes nervously from the back to the front of the stage informing (and sometimes misinforming) his father of the mechanics' progress. After a false announcement he approaches front stage to announce yet another delay. The frame is filled with blackness except for a brightly lighted slit in the curtain just large enough for a face to peer through. In that one moment it seems as though the audience's radiant energy is pouring through and trying to fill the black void of unkept promises, predicting Tucker's final failure.

Vittorio Storaro's credits

The Conformist (1971) Bernardo Bertolucci
Last Tango in Paris (1973) Bernardo Bertolucci
1900 (1977) Bernardo Bertolucci
Apocalypse Now ** (1979) Francis Coppola
Reds ** (1981) Warren Beatty
One from the Heart (1982) Francis Coppola
The Last Emperor ** (1987) Bernardo Bertolucci
Sheltering Sky (1990) Bernardo Bertolucci
The Little Buddha (1994) Bernardo Bertolucci

Tucker:
The Man and His Dream
Dean Tavoularis
Rebuilds Tucker's empire
Production design

"Francis' goal was multi-planed," says Dean Tavoularis, production designer of Francis Coppola's 1940s period film **Tucker: The Man and His Dreams**. "On the superficial level, to have the look of dynamic industrialism, and also of print advertising from the period: a crisp look as opposed to a realistic one." Tavoularis' challenge was to capture the post-World War II media representations of an optimistic, ordered world of progress— a world where all the colors are coordinated, everything is neat, the wife is perfect, it's a perfect sunny day, the dog is perfect, even the placement of the egg on the dish is perfect.

Tavoularis has designed every Francis Coppola film from **The Godfather** in 1972 through **Tucker,** won an Academy Award for its 1974 sequel, and been nominated for two others. In addition to Coppola, his roster of highly respected collaborators includes Arthur Penn, Michelangelo Antonioni and Richard Lester. For **Tucker** Tavoularis and Coppola teamed up for the third time with cinematographer Vittorio Storaro for an 11-week shoot to produce the life story of the 1940s auto maverick, played by Jeff Bridges.

Preston Tucker, who built the world's largest auto plant in the Midwestern U.S. and developed one of the world's most advanced automobiles, had his dream crushed by industry and government opposition. The young Tucker started an ambitious auto sales career and moved quickly up the ladder to larger and more prestigious dealerships. Eventually his ambition outstripped his job status and he formed the Tucker Corporation to compete with the Big Three: Ford, Chrysler, and General Motors. The look of dynamic industrialism was achieved in the numerous scenes set in two location factories: a small three-walled-plus-roof structure which the Tavoularis crew built from scratch, and the full-scale, already existing Ford assembly plant, in which his crew built the manufacturing and assembly line guts of the sets. Contrasting domestic scenes of Tucker at home with his wife (Joan Allen) and children gave Tavoularis the opportunity to evoke the clean '40s print ad look.

Tucker's ultimate demise was brought about by his poor sense of financial planning and the inability to raise the necessary research and development capital, which landed him in Federal Court, accused of illegal fund-raising. Anther example of the antirealistic look Coppola and Tavoularis sought to achieve can be seen in this climactic courtroom scene. "It's not what you would find if you went across the street to the Alameda County (California) Court, explains Tavoularis. "There you'd see a real courtroom, which is very drab by comparison. Our courtroom has a very dramatic look, an unreal look. It's the seat of power, the voice of the government, saying 'I want to talk to you.' It's the power and institutions of the Federal government confronting a small, relatively powerless man."

Dean Tavoularis first heard of Coppola's interest in filming the Tucker story in 1977 while on location in the Philippines for **Apocalypse Now**. Coppola had prepared a script from preliminary research into Preston Tucker's life and automobile. The project was shelved until the mid-1980s, about the time a biography, **The Indomitable Tin Goose** by former Tucker PR man Charles T. Pearson, was published and used as the basis of a new script by Arnold Schulman.

In late 1986 and early '87 **Tucker**'s pre-production team held a series of meetings in California. The team consisted of Coppola, Storaro, Tavoularis, executive producer George Lucas, producer Fred Fuchs, and occasionally Schulman, costume designer Milena Canonero, and set designer Alex Tavoularis, who is Dean's brother and long-time collaborator. During the course of these meetings, script revisions occurred and production schedules and shooting locations were determined. Major locations included a rural Sonoma County setting for Tucker's multi-storied Midwestern home and small factory, and urban locales for the large Tucker factory and courtroom scenes. The old Ford assembly plant was chosen not least because of its vast full-length skylight, which eased Storaro's lighting problems considerably.

These production/script meetings and the script itself served as the basis of the storyboards, which were the all-important common point of reference and consultation for the production team members. "As sets were being designed, a sketch artist drew storyboards based on our production meetings," says Tavoularis. "We designed the sets in the order of shooting. We had shot over half the film by the time the storyboards were actually finished." In the interests of efficiency, the production team decided to build the small factory from the bottom up, within a few hundred feet of the already existing Tucker home. This offered cinematographer Storaro a good deal of flexibility in panning and dollying from house to factory. In order to have the factory structure ready to meet the film's shooting schedule—which was as much as possible in the script order of continuity—the crew worked nonstop, pouring the foundation and erecting the three-walled building with attached roof in a brief two weeks.

While the production meetings were in progress, Dean

213

Tavoularis also spent two weeks steeping himself in Tucker lore—reading transcripts of interviews with the car's designer (Alex Tremulis), listening to audio cassette interviews with Tucker family members and enthusiasts, poring over still shots of the Tucker automobile, viewing an original Tucker Corporation sales promotional film; and reading period magazine articles on the Tucker. The promotional film was made by Tucker in the 1940s to inform his national sales staff of the car's many revolutionary features, such as a centrally located headlight that turned in tandem with and in the same direction as the steering wheel. A blowup of this original 16mm promo film is frequently intercut in **Tucker** with the restaged and reshot version of the original.

Dean Tavoularis regards the process of setting up his production office—in this case central to most of the location at the Marin Lucasfilm headquarters—as integral to the creative process of production design. And it is no small wonder, considering the next lengthy task he had before him in carrying out **Tucker's** production design: assembling "the lists." The lists were comprised of everything his department of 40 would work with: props (on-camera magazines and newspapers, sketches, and illustrations of car designs), stock footage, locations, research materials; lists of Tucker owners to contact, Tucker company emblems, banners, shields. More than 30 of the approximately 50 existing Tucker automobiles in the U.S. were brought to the Bay area for this shoot He points out that this process is the same for all the features on which he works, it's the contents of the lists that varies.

With the filmmaking team as intentionally collaborative as Coppola's, a production design decision can affect the way the story is told. An example of this on **Tucker** was a phone booth conversation sequence, which involved two settings, and was originally scheduled to be shot at different times and locations. Tavoularis describes the sequence: "Tucker is in the factory, driving around one of his cars. He gets a telephone call, goes over to the telephone and it's his business partner, Abe, who's in a phone booth. He's telling Tucker, 'You better get out of the factory because the police are looking for you and they're going to come to arrest you and make a big show.'"

Tavoularis says the shots of Tucker answering the phone were scheduled to be filmed with the factory scenes, and that the shots of Abe at a phone booth were to be filmed later, with other material on the streets. Tavoularis continues, "Francis told me that he wanted to experiment doing telephone conversations together rather than cutting between different shots. Sometimes in those old films you have a split screen where one guy is on the left, another on the right; to accomplish this, different shots are optically married together—to avoid all that cutting. They never do that anymore, because it's kind of an old-fashioned thing.

"So in this case I went ahead and planned for Abe to be in a little diner, with it dark and raining outside. And Tucker's in a factory in the daylight. But I physically put these things together; the set were constructed next to one another, and shot on one set at the same time." Costly setup time and expenses were saved because fewer cameras setups were required and all the shooting for what previously were two locations could now be done at one site at one time. The concept of combining locations and separate scenes physically to be shot at the same time is an innovation, one not only as a production design device, but also as a narrative one. Through its use, marriage of image, concept, and locale takes place.

On a more symbolic note, Tavoularis describes how one of the central motifs of the picture came about: "One of the characters says to Preston Tucker as he's leaving a meeting, 'I'll see you in Chicago.' To which Tucker responds, "Yeah, if you want to have a ringside seat at your own crucifixion.'

"The next scene shows Tucker watching the name sign going up over his new factory. Instead of having the sign go up, I said, 'Let's just put the letter "T" and a connecting device to lift it up as it's being set on top of the building.' The 'UCKER' is already on top of the building. So when he says, 'You'll have a ringside seat at your own crucifixion,' you see this letter—which now becomes like a cross—being craned up the building.

"There are a lot of interesting moments that we conceived like that one—that's what you do when you design a movie. You say, 'Let's do it that way. Let's not do it that way.' So we thought of a way to make it more dramatic."

Dean Tavoularis sums up his philosophy by saying that the production designer should be involved at both the highest overview level as well as at the lowest design levels. "I think production design is this overview. I would feel very uncomfortable—and I think some people do work like that—to be way up there and always be on overview, and not be concerned about what goes on below. I think you create the overview by working on the bottom. It's like a plant that has this root system that flowers out on top."

GLOSSARY

BACKGROUND NOISE: the surrounding noises behind the dialogue or major sounds of a scene, tacked on to a scene to give atmosphere or added realism.

BOOM MAN, BOOM OPERATOR: the sound expert who operates the boom and its attendant microphone.

DAILIES: (aka rushes) the first copies of the day's shooting prints usually made from camera original, shown with dialogue synch sound.

DIALOGUE: the spoken part of the sound track usually shown in synch with picture.

DISTORTION: any alteration in a sound signal that makes it lose its original distinctness and character.

EFFECTS: (aka FXs) noises added after the shooting of an action, for example, a gunshot, a storm, or footsteps.

FOLEY: any human motion sound or sound effect that is recorded in a studio as the images for a scene are run, and is then cut into the picture. For example, in a foot race scene, a Foley expert would watch the scene to be Foleyed and play the actions of the actor while making believable sounds (footsteps, heavy breathing).

LIMITER: an amplifier device that keeps signals from surpassing a stipulated limit.

LOOPING: (aka ADR) the procedure of recording dialogue to fit the previously recorded lip movements of the performer. When the language is not the same as was used in the original film the process is termed dubbing.

MIXING: the procedure of coalescing sound tracks, encompassing fades, cross fades, volume adjustments, and equalizations.

MIXER, PRODUCTION: head sound recordist on the set whose first responsibility is to realize the best recorded sound practicable throughout production.

MIXER, RERECORDING: the principal sound engineer accountable for the final mix when all of the disparate sound tracks, including dialogue, music and all effects tracks are combined and balanced to make the picture's final sound track.

SCRATCH MIX: (aka slop mix) one of the first sound mixes used in cutting the film before the final mix is made. The scratch mix combines dialogue and certain sound effects or music without any effort at rectifying sound.

Further Reading

Alten, Stanley R., *Audio in Media*, Belmont, California: Wadsworth, 1981

Antheil, George, *Bad Boy of Music*, New York, 1945

Antheil, George, "New Tendencies in Composing for Films," *Film Culture*, I/4, p. 16

Altman, Rick, editor, *Sound Theory, Sound Practice*, New York: Routledge, 1992

Alwyn, W., "How Not to Write Film Music," *British Film Academy Journal* (1954), autumn, p. 7

Alwyn, W., "Composing for the Screen," *Films and Filming*, v/6 (1959), pp. 9, 34

Amyes, Tim. *The Technique Of Audio Post-production In Video And Film*, London, Boston: Focal Press, 1990

Bazelon, I., *Knowing the Score: Notes on Film Music*, New York, 1975

Bernstein, Elmer, (editor), "An interview with Hugo Friedhofer," *Filmmusic Notebook* i, (1974), pp. 12-21

Bernstein, Elmer, "On Film Music," *Journal of the University Film Association*, xxviii/4 (1976) p. 7

Bernstein, Elmer, (editor), "A Conversation with Leo Shuken," *Filmmusic Notebook*, spring, 1975, p. 14

Bernstein, Elmer, "Whatever happened to Great Movie Music," *High Fidelity and Musical America*, Vol. 22, no. 7, (July, 1972)

Blake, Larry, *Film Sound Today: An Anthology Of Articles From Recording Engineer/Producer*, Hollywood, California: Reveille Press, 1984

Bookspan, M. and R. Yockey, *Andre Previn*, New York and London, 1981

Cameron, K., *Sound and the Documentary Film*, London, 1947

Caps, J., "Interview with Jerome Moross," *Cue Sheet* v/3,4 (1988)

Carroll, B., *Erich Wolfgang Korngold 1897-1957, His Life and Works*, Paisley, Scotland, 1984

Chion, Michel, *Audio-vision: Sound on Screen*; edited and translated by Claudia Gorbman; with a foreword by Walter Murch, New York: Columbia University Press, 1994

Darby, K., "Alfred Newman Biography and Filmography," *Filmmusic Notebook* ii (1976) pp. 5-13

Deutsch, A., "Collaboration Between the Screen Writer and the Composer," *Proceedings of the Writers' Congress*, Los Angeles, 1944

Elley, D. (editor), "Dimitri Tiomkin: the Man and His Music," *National Film Dossier No. 1* (1986)

Evans, Mark, *Soundtrack: The Music Of The Movies*, New York: Da Capo Press, 1979

Faulkner, R.R., *Hollywood Studio Musicians*, Chicago, 1971

Forlenza, Jeff and Terri Stone (Mix Magazine), editors, *Sound For Picture: An Inside Look At Audio Production For Film And Television*, foreword by Francis Coppola, Milwaukee, Wisconsin: Hal Leonard Publishing Corporation, 1993

Frater, C., *Sound Recording for Motion Pictures*, Cranbury, New Jersey, 1975

Frayne, John G., Ph.D., *Elements of Sound Recording*, New York: John Wiley and Sons, Inc., 1949

Freeland, M. (editor), *Composed and Conducted by Walter Scharf*, London and New Jersey, 1988

Hagen, Earl, *Scoring for Films*, New York: Wehman, 1972

Herrmann, Bernard, "Score for a Film" in *Focus On Citizen Kane*, edited by Ronald Gottesman, Englewood Cliffs, New Jersey: Prentice-Hall, Inc., 1971

Herrmann, Bernard, "The Colour of the Music," *Sight and Sound*, xli (1972). p. 36 [interview]

Honore, Paul M., *A Handbook Of Sound Recording: A Text For Motion Picture And General Sound Recording;* with foreword and final chapter on The art of presentation by Hal Honore, South Brunswick, New Jersey: A. S. Barnes, 1980

Hubatka, Milton C. Frederick Hull, and Richard W. Sanders; editor, Vincent L. Wolfe, *Audio Sweetening For Film And TV*, Blue Ridge Summit, Pennsylvania: TAB Professional and Reference Books, 1985

Huntley, John, and Roger Manvell, *The Technique of Film Music*, London: Focal Press, 1957

Kellogg, Edward W., "The ABC of Photographic Sound Recording," Journal of the Society of Motion Picture Engineers, vol. 44, March, 1945, No. 3, pp. 151-194 [probably the best explanation of optical sound reproduction, still the global standard (with some modifications) for theatrical motion picture exhibition]

Kellogg, Edward W., "History of Sound Motion Pictures," Journal of the SMPTE, August, 1955, vol. 64, no. 8, pp. 422-437

Kerner, Marvin M., *The Art Of The Sound Effects*, Boston: Focal Press, 1989

Limbacher, J. L., (editor) *Film Music*, Metuchen, New Jersey, 1974

LoBrutto, Vincent, *Sound-on-film: Interviews With Creators Of Film Sound*, Westport, Connnecticut: Praeger, 1994

Lustig, Milton, *Music Editing For Motion Pictures*, New York: Hastings House, 1980

McCarty, C. (editor), *Film Music l*, New York and London, 1989

Mott, Robert L., *Sound Effects: Radio, TV, And Film*, Boston: Focal Press, 1990

Myerson, Harold and Ernest Harburg, *Who Put the Rainbow in the **Wizard** of Oz: Lyricist Yip Harburg*, Ann Arbor: University of Michigan Press, 1993, 1995

Nisbit, Alec, *The Sound Studio*, Oxford University Press, New York: 1995

Ohanian, Thomas A., *Digital Nonlinear Editing*, Boston: Focal Press, 1993

Prendergast, R.M., *A Neglected Art: A Critical Study of Music in Films*, New York, 1977

Skiles, Marlin, *Music Scoring for TV and Motion Pictures*, Tab Books, Blue Ridge Summit, Pennsylvania 17214, 1976

Skinner, F. *Underscore* (New York, 1960), [textbook on film scoring]

Stein, Fred, "Hermann's 'Black and White' Music for Hitchcock's **Psycho**," *Elmer Bernstein's Film Music Collection*, Vol. 1 (Fall, 1974), p. 31

Weis, Elisabeth and John Belton, editors, *Film Sound*, New York: Columbia University Press, 1985

Woram, John M., *The Recording Studio Handbook*, Plainview, New York 11803: ELAR, 1982.

Zaza, Anthony James, *Audio Design: The Narrative Functions Of Sound*, Beverly Hills, California: Moss Publications, distributed by Crosscountry Film/Video, 1985

Zaza, Anthony James, *Audio Design: Sound Recording Techniques For Film And Video*, Englewood Cliffs, New Jersey: Prentice-Hall: 1991

Trade Magazines

AES: Journal of the Audio Engineering Society,
    New York, New York
American Cinematographer, Hollywood, California
Mix Magazine, Emeryville, California
Journal of the SMPTE, Scarsdale, New York
Studio Sound, London, England

Index

CCD (charge coupled device
    archival sound restoration, 192
China
    The Last Emperor
        Sharrock, Ivan, 53
Cinecittà
    Sharrock, Ivan, 53
communicating with....
    postproduction, 62
completely filled track
    foreign
        post production recording, 186
concert filming
    The Doors, 72
Coppola, Francis, 88, 93, See also **Apocalypse Now, Cotton Club,**
    Gardens of Stone, One From The Heart, Tucker
Cotton Club, 135
    Richard Beggs
        Francis Coppola, 127
creative interaction, 131
    Cotton Club, See Coppola, Francis
    D.C. Cab
        director (working with), 132
cue tracks
    music, 26

D

dailies, 40
dancing
    A Chorus Line, 25
DAWs
    digital audio workstations, 199
dialogue, 60, 66, 72, 91
    Mosquito Coast, 107
    production mixing
        production recording, 25
digital compatibility standards
    DAWs
        digital audio workstations, 200
digital metronome (aka thumper)
    A Chorus Line, 28
digital reverb device
    Lexicon 224XL Lark

probe vocalizations
  whale song
    Star Trek IV: The Long Voyage Home, 165
production recording
  production mixing, 60, 65, 67, 68, 78, 82, 134, 135
    monestaries, 67, 68

Q

quality of film sound, the, 84

R

racing boats used for location shooting
  Wind
    Ballard, Carroll, 45
radio mikes
  in helmets
    Platoon, 64
  production recording
    location recording, 34, 48
recording
  applause, 96
  explosion, 60
  flatulence
    Amadeus, 98
  gunfire
    Platoon, 60
  jungle sounds
    Platoon, 61
  war picture
    Platton, 61
recording and....
  creative expression, 94
recording for....
  theatrical versus broadcast television
    Nelson Stoll, 79
recording location sound, 60
recording materials
  quarter-inch tapes of dialogue, 94
recording with...
  multiple cameras, 73
  live instruments, 72
release formats

About the author:

Nicholas Pasquariello has been writing internationally about the more technical aspects of filmmaking for more than two decades for a wide variety of trade magazines and other publications including *American Cinematographer*, *Mix*, *On Location*, *LOCATIONS*, *Chaplin*, *Premiere*, *Producer Magazine*, *Millimeter*, *ACTION*, *Filmmakers Newsletter*, the *San Francisco Chronicle*, *Videography*, *Video Systems*, *BROADCAST*, and *USA Today*.